Processionals, Props, & Pageantry

Other Books By The Author

Dancing for Him
Dancing for the Lord during praise and worship, ministry, and presentations

Dance, Dance, Dance!
A scriptural reference guide to the English, Hebrew, and Greek words related to movement

Team Terrificus
Tips & techniques with the fruit of the Spirit for leaders' and member's success.

Creative Worship
Many ideas for creative cohesiveness and coordinated effort.

Prophetic Dance
Learning to express the Father's heart through movement.

Divine Choreography
Divine Inspirations: Choreography Technique

Dance In The Church, What's The Pointe?
An honest look at honest questions.

Processionals, Props, & Pageantry

By Lynn M. Hayden

Scriptural significance & Practical Guide

♥ SECOND EDITION 2005, THIRD EDITION 2008

ISBN-10: 0-9771925-0-4
ISBN-13: 978-0-9771925-0-2

Layout and cover design Jessica Mitchem
Book Production: SPS Publications
www.spsbooks.com

Dedication

To my mom and dad, who so graciously afforded me a lovely, quiet place to write.

Table of contents

INTRODUCTION

Magnificence of His presence abounds as worshippers process. Flags flown in adoration to the King of glory radiate resplendence. Pageantry prepared for the Lord shines with Splendor. "Processionals, Props, and Pageantry" was born from the wonderment of such.

I began teaching and participating in processionals many years ago, during which time, I developed curiosity about their scriptural significance. After much research, I then wanted to provide a resource or reference guide to others that covered not only the scriptural significance, but also the practical usage aspects.

The book is divided into three parts: Processionals, Props, and Pageantry, respectively. Each section has two parts. The first two chapters in each part (Scriptural Significance) contain many scriptures validating the particular chapter topic. The second two chapters in that part (Practical Guide) discuss many tips and ideas that any dancer, worshipper, or team leader may use as a foundation from which to fashion a myriad of ideas.

My hope is that you enjoy the testimonies, learn about the scriptural significance, and wear out the pages in the practical guide. I trust that this book will give you a sufficient foundation from which to build countless processionals that have resplendence, magnificence, and splendor!

Part one: Processionals

Scriptural Significance

Practical Guide

Psalm 68:24-26- They have seen Your procession, O God, the procession of my God, my King, into the sanctuary. Vs. 25 The singers went before, the players on instruments followed after; among them were the maidens playing timbrels. Bless God in the congregations, the Lord, from the fountain of Israel.

Since God inhabits the praises of His people, and we as worshippers, praise Him through our movement (see the Dance, Dance, Dance! book), then as we process into the sanctuary, we usher in His presence. This may or may not be done with timbrels (specifically), but we can bless God in the congregation, and change the whole atmosphere of a meeting.

In the first two chapters, I would simply like to present and highlight some of the scriptures that relate to procession. Some Hebrew words reveal the topic from which I hope you will gain greater appreciation and understanding. Then, I want to highlight some practical aspects.

Scriptural Significance

Chapter 1: Care to Go For A Walk?

Joshua 1:3 – "Every place that the sole of your foot will tread upon I have given you, as I said to Moses. Vs. 5 No man shall be able to stand before you all the days of your life; as I was with Moses, so I will be with you. I will not leave you nor forsake you."

What comforting words. These promises can not only support us in our personal daily walk, but also as we stroll down an aisle in procession. As we worship, while going (through the sanctuary), we know that He will never leave us or forsake us. This can be rather comforting, especially to the person who has never been in a presentation or processional.

Every place that our feet tread He has given us. That sounds like victory over the enemy. If while we process, we believe that we can take back that which the enemy has stolen for others (in the pews), and ourselves, then certainly, a processional can be more then a pretty pageant. Healing, and deliverance can happen to the faith-filled believer through the simple act of going for a walk.

The following Hebrew word (found in several scriptures) should illustrate, in more depth, the importance of a walking movement or procession.

HALIYKAH OR HALIJKAH—Walking, moving or marching in a procession, caravan, or traveling company; a march; a going; way.[1]

Haliykah (which is in scripture) means walking. If walking is movement and movement is dance, then a walking movement (or processional dance) is scriptural. Let us look at a few verses. I commented on some and made bold the corresponding English interpretations.

*Job 6:19 – The **caravans** of Tema looked, the **travelers** of Sheba waited for them.*

*Psalms 68:24 – They have seen your **procession**, O God; the **procession** of my God, my King, in the sanctuary.*

*Proverbs 31:27 – She looks well to the **ways** of her household, and eats not the bread of idleness.*

Even moving in silence, doing normal household activities gives glory to God and confounds the enemy.

*Nahum 2:5 – He shall recount his Nobles; they shall stumble in their **walk**; they shall make haste to the wall there of, and the defense shall be prepared.*

*Habakkuk 3:6 – He stood, and measured the earth; he beheld, and drove asunder the nations; and the everlasting mountains were scattered, the perpetual hills did bow; his **ways** are everlasting.*

There is power in movement. God looked and startled

the nations and the mountains were scattered. Hills even bowed. His ways are everlasting. God's movements are so powerful (when He moves in a procession) that even the mountains respond to His glance. How powerful against the enemy is our movement when the all-powerful God is resident with in us?!

Some other scriptures pertain to walking or marching. Let us look at those.

Psalm 24:7 – Lift up your heads, O you gates! And be lifted up, you everlasting doors! And the King of glory ***shall come in****.*

While a congregation waits inside the gates, a king and his procession ask if they may enter. In the later verses, the gatekeeper asks for identification to which the king replies, Vs. 8 "The Lord strong and mighty, the Lord mighty in battle." Once verification of identity is established, He may enter.

The Lord wants to *process* into our hearts as well as our sanctuaries. If we open our hearts (the ventricle-type inner chambers of hurt or pain) and open our church doors (that have been shut to that which has only been undiscovered) then His glory will come in. Where there is *His* light there is no darkness. He is able to heal that broken heart and shed light in the congregation as a glittering chorus of worshippers jubilantly express His healing balm and beauty.

2 Corinthians 2:14-16 – Now thanks be to God who always leads us in ***triumph*** *in Christ, and through us diffuses the fragrance of His knowledge in every place. 15. For we are to God the fragrance of Christ among those who are being saved and among those who are perishing. 16. To the one, we are the aroma of death leading to death, and to the other the aroma of* *life leading to life. And who is sufficient for these things?*

"The Roman triumph was a victory parade for a conquering army and its leader. Both victors and captives were part of the procession, and both groups could smell the fragrance of burning spices, which accompanied the parade. The aroma, however, meant something different to the two groups. Likewise, the fragrance of Christ (the gospel) is to those who are perishing an aroma of death leading to death, for it signifies and leads to their ultimate judgment. Those who are being saved find the knowledge of Christ to be an aroma of life leading to life, for it signifies life now and leads to life eternal." [2]

The gospel presentation done through our processional interpretation can be an aroma of life. It could be the catalyst that brings those, who once saw a death march, to salvation. So significant is the serious nature of people's destinies contained within the Christian. As we walk down the aisle in a beautiful parade of triumph, we can actually emit the fragrance of Christ, an aroma that sets captives free!

Scriptural Significance

Chapter 2: Let's have a feast!

Exodus 12:14 – And this day shall be unto you for a memorial; and you shall ***keep it a feast*** *to the Lord throughout your generations; you shall* ***keep it a feast*** *by an ordinance for ever.*

In remembrance of Passover, God orders a convocation or sacred assembly. This is a feast calling together people for rest and worship. Gathering in sacred assembly (like a procession) to observe this feast, honors the Lord.

As you will see on the next page, the Hebrew word associated with keeping a feast means dancing in sacred procession (among other things). Therefore, it is wonderful to know that every time this word is associated with a feast in the scriptures (and there are many feasts), it is analogous with festive dancing!

CHAGAG (cha-gagh) – FEAST – A sacred celebration, marching in a sacred procession; to keep a feast; to be festive; assemble for rejoicing and celebration; reeling to and fro; dancing in a sacred procession; similar to qatar or qetoreth – a fumigation that drives out the occupants and causes deliverance; to celebrate; to move in a circle; to dance; to make a pilgrimage; keep a pilgrim feast; to observe a festival; keep or hold a solemn feast or holiday; idea of leaping.[1]

I again, made bold the corresponding scriptures related to chagag.

*Exodus 5:1 – And afterward Moses and Aaron went in, and told Pharaoh, thus says the Lord God of Israel, Let my people go, that they may hold a **feast** unto me in the wilderness.*

*Exodus 23:14 – Three times will you **keep a feast** unto me in the year.*

*Leviticus 23:41 – And you shall **keep it a feast** unto the Lord seven days in the year. It shall be a statute forever in your generations: you shall celebrate it in the seventh month.*

"The name Haggai comes from **chagag** and means *Festive One* or *Celebrating One.* The Old Testament abounds in feasts and celebrations, ordained by God and resulting in human happiness. Feasting was a time of resting from common tasks and dwelling on God's mercy and grace."[2]

*Leviticus 23:39 – Also in the fifteenth day of the seventh month, when you have gathered in the fruit of the land, you shall **keep a feast** unto the Lord seven days: on the first day shall be a Sabbath, and on the eighth day shall be a Sabbath.*

After the work or harvest is complete for a season, there is a time for rest, and then again, Sabbath rest, as

God commands. It is interesting that this rest includes dancing.

Numbers 29:12 – And on the fifteenth day of the seventh month, you shall have an holy convocation; you shall do no servile work, and you shall ***keep a feast*** *unto the Lord seven days.*

All the way down through verse 40, as an act of worship, they brought many different kinds of offerings to the Lord. Now, as we march in a procession as an act of worship before our King, we are offering ourselves up to Him as a living sacrifice.

I Samuel 30:16 – And when he had brought him down, behold, they were spread abroad upon all the earth, eating and drinking, and ***dancing****, because of all the great spoil that they had taken out of the land of the Philistines, and out of the land of Judah.*

In the enemy's camp, there is always a counterfeit. They were celebrating and dancing because of their supposed victory over the Philistines and the land of Judah. However, it was not long afterward that the Mighty One of Israel defeated their camp and took back that which the enemy had stolen.

Nahum 1:15 – Behold upon the mountains the feet of him that brings good tidings, that publishes peace! O Judah, ***keep thy solemn feasts****, perform thy vows: for the wicked shall no more pass through thee; he is utterly cut off.*

A perfume of fire is released to God when praising Him in a holy procession. The result in the spirit realm is that when we offer praise to the Lord or when we "Chagag" Him, the enemy of our souls is utterly cut off!

Psalms 42:4 – When I remember these things, I pour out my soul in me; for I had gone with the multitude, I went with them to the house of God, with the voice of joy and praise, with a multitude that ***kept holy day.***

That **kept holy day** (kept a pilgrim feast) has the important derivative CHAG (feast), which especially refers to the seven feasts God gave to Israel. Worship and praise was very important in OT times and should be that much more important now since we have Jesus Christ! This type of joy (rinnah) is a shout of rejoicing or cheering in triumph at a time of victory over the defeat or elimination of the wicked.[2]

Deuteronomy 16:15 – "Seven days you shall ***keep a sacred feast*** *to the Lord your God in the place which the Lord chooses, because the Lord your God will bless you in all your produce and in all the work of your hands, so that you surely rejoice."*

This verse later goes on to explain that when the males bring an offering to these feasts (three times a year – Feast of Unleavened Bread, Feast of Weeks, and the Feast of Tabernacles) that they will not come empty handed. The Lord promises to bless and provide. God wants our praise. He wants us to gather, as in a "procession" to worship, honor, and adore. Let's have a feast!

Practical Guide

Chapter 3: Prayer, Planning, and Practice

Joshua 6 – Vs. 2 And the Lord said to Joshua: "See! I have given Jericho into your hand, its king, and the mighty men of valor. Vs. 3 You shall march around the city, all you men of war; you shall go all around the city once. This you shall do six days…"

The rest of the chapter describes in detail, how to go around the city and what to do to be victorious! This is probably one of the most unusual movement patterns that God (the greatest choreographer) directed. He could have instructed them to go around three times, completely surround it after the third time, back away from the wall, and then charge it while laughing. He could have instructed them to go around it one time forward, one time backward, then walk away from it ten paces, kneel down and worship. The important point is not how many times to go around and in which direction, or what instrument they should play and what kind of exclamation they should utter. It is that God instructed, they obeyed, and there was victory!

It is important that we carefully listen to God's instructions, be obedient, and march to the cadence of His drum in order to gain victorious ground and usher in His presence.

Although, it seems that processionals would be the easiest type of dances for which to prepare, they often require the most **prayer, planning, and practice**. This is particularly true if you incorporate complicated patterns. In this section, I would like to give you some *basic ideas* for laying a foundation. You may use these as templates from which to build your own Spirit-inspired processional designs filled with splendor, brilliance and majesty.

Start with **prayer**, whether you are asked by your leadership to prepare a piece for a particular occasion/ holiday, or you have the liberty to present what you have when you have it. If your leadership asked or expected you to do a particular piece, the prayers need to be about whom, what, and how. On the other hand, if you have total responsibility and liberty, the prayers may be who, what, how, *and when*. Sometimes, you may have a wonderful idea or inspiration, but the possibility for doing it at another time or season is worth extra prayerful deliberation.

Once you have prayed and gotten sufficient answers to your questions, then it is time to **plan**. The Lord usually gives me a basic outline of a dance or processional, over which I mull recurrently. I listen to the music successively. My friends often jest that we only listen to twelve songs a year. I often write down the words and/or counts accordingly and get to know the music inside out and backwards. It is always a good idea to write everything down. We are all fallible humans who may forget on occasion. Therefore, it is good to have your reference notes available.

Write it down and make it plain

Diagram 1

1	2
3	4
5	6
7	8

Then, it is befitting to put the basic choreography ideas into the appropriate squares. Not everyone is able to read my notes. Some may think I should have been a football coach with all the markings, and arrows covering the page. One person questioned me, years ago: "you learned about all those little X's and O's in college"? Certainly, you can develop your own symbols, but this is what has worked for me over the years.

Next, I divide many pieces of paper into about eight quadrants each (**Diagram 1**). I number each quadrant, and insert corresponding words or music phrases from the song. Primarily, these are notes written for myself, however, it is not a bad idea to pen them legibly enough so that others can read them. One time, I was in the middle of doing a large dance, and had to minister out for a couple of weeks. Rather then canceling all the practices, I handed my notes over to my assistant (to which she adhered adeptly) and she handled the practices beautifully.

Symbol	Item	Names
X	Dances	Mary/Cathy Cindy/ Amy
O	Hoops	Michele/ Chris Dan
	Large Banners	Fred/ Jody
	Streamers	Linda/ Lisa
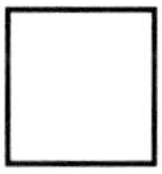	Large Flags	Candy/Karen Barbara/Tom

Diagram 2

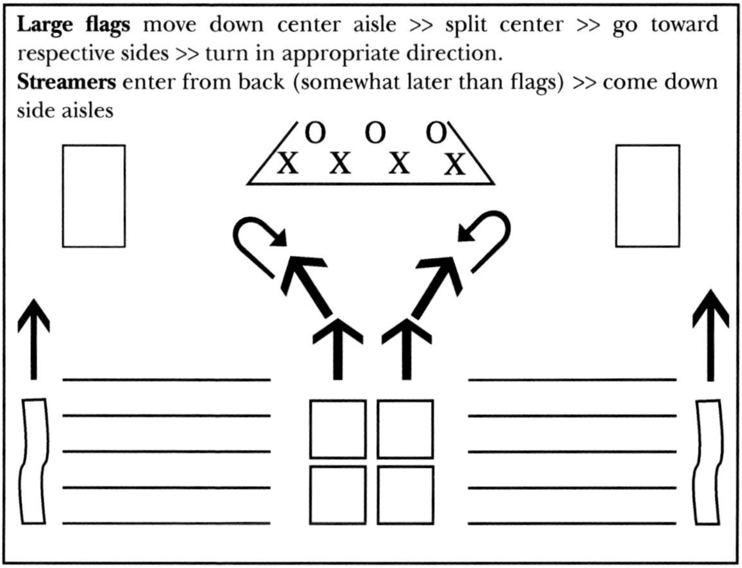

Large flags move down center aisle >> split center >> go toward respective sides >> turn in appropriate direction.
Streamers enter from back (somewhat later than flags) >> come down side aisles

Diagram 3

I usually designate an X for each of the dancers who enter initially. People who carry flags are usually indicated by a small square. Large rectangles are reserved for the bearers of large banners, and O's are used for other dancers or prop bearers who enter later. If it is more complex, I either increase/decrease the size of the figures, or add different ones altogether. Sometimes, I just use squares and put the initials of the dancers in it. I have included a basic sample of a legend **(diagram 2)** and a very simple display of a movement phrase in a blow-up of one of the choreography squares **(diagram 3)**.

Diagram 3 depicts the large banners, hoops, and dancers already in their places. This particular square shows only the movement pattern of the large flags and the streamers. The large flags come down the aisle two by two, split center front, move toward their respective sides and then circle to the left or right (depending on what side they are). At this point, the streamers are only making their entrance from the back of the sanctuary and coming down the side aisles somewhat after the large flags. In the space above the stage, I usually write the counts and choreography for that section. When the choreography is different for the flags, hoops, and dancers, during the same phrase of music, I simply create duplicate squares for the individual groups. It is not essential to compress a lot of choreography in one small square. Taking the time to spread it out is worth the effort.

Diagramming is a very helpful part of laying a foundation for a powerful processional. However, another part of planning, that I usually do, is go to the church building or facility where the processional is to be done and walk it out by myself. Sometimes, I just let the music play while I sit and envision the whole thing. Other times, I walk out individuals' parts to see how long it may take them to get down the aisle and get to certain spots. It's a good idea to have your "ducks in a row" or "O's in a line before you actually have a rehearsal. It makes the practices run much smoother.

Concerning **practice**, do it repeatedly, if possible. After you have prayed, and 'planned your work', then it's time to 'work your plan'. Some of these basic practice tips are maneuvers that I have successfully executed over the years that should help you with your rehearsals.

1. It is a good idea, after team prayer, to let everyone hear the music.
2. Line them up or place them accordingly in the front of the sanctuary and on the stage where most of the activity will take place.
3. Have them exit in reverse order toward the area from which they will enter. For example, (using diagram 3):
    a. The large banners would exit to the left and right.
    b. The flags would go down the center aisle

(in reverse order from where they will come in).

c. The dancers and hoops would likewise retreat down the sides of the stage and then down the center aisle (hoops being the last ones out).

In other words, it is good to work backward in the beginning so their entrance will be smooth and so the correct people will end up in the right places. Done correctly, the line-up in the back of the church should be:

Hoops
Dancers
Flags
Streamers waiting by the side aisles
Large banners waiting at the sides of the front.

4. Go through ¼ - ½ of the dance (or as much as you feel confident) without music. Simply to get them comfortable with their movement patterns (where they go and after whom).
5. Do a very small segment of processing with the music. It builds their confidence and gives everyone a sense of accomplishment when a little is done well. Do not be discouraged at this point, however, if the timing or positioning is not absolutely where you want it. It is only a matter of minor readjustment and you will be right on track.
6. Simply continue in like manner until the dance is complete or time runs out (which ever comes first).
7. Close in prayer.

It ***is*** possible to orchestrate a processional without much planning or practice, and the anointing covers a multitude of mistakes. Nevertheless, I personally prefer, whenever possible, to practice sufficiently enough that the dancers feel so confident with their patterns, movements, and steps, that they would not even have to think about them. While they are doing the movements, they *should be able to worship,* not worry.

There have been occasions where I have had to produce large productions with very little allotted practice time in the presentation space. One time that was particularly challenging was when I had a total of about 48 minutes to teach 48 non-English speaking Koreans a processional to a song they had never heard in an enormous sanctuary that I had never seen. I felt like a ground crew flagging in five jumbo-jets for a simultaneous landing. The result was that none of them crashed, all the gear was intact, and the anointing actually fell!

After obediently dancing to God's drumbeat, the endeavor will be worth the prayer, planning, and practice. There is much gratification when the unified team is able to worship wholly, usher in the presence of God, and do the presentation with a spirit of excellence. However, beside these combined elements, there is nothing comparable to ministering to the Lord, and the hearts of people, thereby gaining victorious ground!

Practical Guide

Chapter 4: Positioning & Patterns

II Chronicles 20:17&22 – You will not need to fight in this battle. Position yourselves, stand still and see the salvation of the Lord, who is with you, O Judah and Jerusalem! Do not fear or be dismayed; tomorrow go out against them, for the Lord is with you." Vs. 22 Now when they began to sing and praise, the Lord set ambushes against the people of Ammon, Moab, and Mount Seir, who had come against Judah; and they were defeated.

It is important that we position ourselves properly in the middle of God's will, even if that happens to be in a processional. If we are in tune with His Spirit, and obedient to His Word, we (and those to whom we minister) will be abundantly blessed. The purpose of this chapter is to give basic pattern and positioning ideas from which your wellspring of ideas may be birthed. There are probably as many patterns and positions as there are stars in the sky. It is my goal to stimulate your thinking and activate your creativity so the artistry that Holy Spirit produces through you will be exhilarating and life changing.

Concerning the entrance, beginning, or introduction, most processionals start from the back of the church and caravan forward to the front, ushering in the presence of the Lord. There is one small problem with that, however, unless you have a semi-circular, 3-5 thousand seat auditorium, the splendor and anointing of the large labor-intensive banners may not be perceived or received to their fullest potential. There are some simple solutions to this dilemma. One is to have the beautiful, large banners come down the side aisles, turning them inward to face the congregation (I will expound on this in chapter 7). Another is to have them start from off-stage (behind the curtains) if the facility is large enough. If the function is being held in a civic center, there is plenty of room to enter from behind and beside the stage.

Also, especially in a smaller, more traditional church setting, they could be stationed before the dance begins, in the front corners of the sanctuary. These banners could begin to move across the front and/or down the aisles, which could be done in addition to or instead of what is happening on the stage. However, since the large banners are so grand and majestic, saving them for a more powerful portion of the song, may be worth consideration.

Another problem with starting the entire processional from the back is that for the first sixteen counts, or so, of introductory music, the audience is unaware of what is going on. In some cases, however, those who are aware, crane their necks to watch what is going on. One solution is to start with a dancer or two on the stage. The audience will focus their attention on that which is moving the most. Therefore, since they are facing forward, and their eyes are forward, then their attention will be on the stage (whatever type of movement you decide is befitting). Then, as the procession emerges from the back, the impact will be that much greater. In a recent Christmas special, I did just that. The song was "Silent Night" by Twila Paris. I ran in and did a simple solo for the introduction and part of the first verse. Meanwhile, a procession of worshippers, holding battery-operated candles, entered from the back (down the side aisles) of the darkened sanctuary. They then made two continuously moving lines on the stage forming a large semi-circle "'round yon virgin" (me). After they went off the stage, they picked up several large five yard worship cloths and processed back down the aisles. By this time, however (during the transition), two other dancers joined me on the stage. The dance then grew in intensity. If we had just started the processional with only the candles, we would have run into the problems I mentioned earlier. This one, simple idea added interest, another dimension, and an interpretive story line.

Good spacing (positioning) can only be accomplished with practice. It is necessary to watch how far apart each dancer is from another (especially during the entrance) to create uniformity and good visual line. We tend to think of processionals as being slow and majestic. In most cases, this is true, common, and widely accepted. This form is good to introduce dance in a church. Even the most conservative churches usually appreciate the magnificence of this type of reverential honor bestowed upon the Lord. However, we do not have to be confined by this format. I have seen, taught, and participated in processionals done to lively, upbeat, or victorious music, that were well received and anointed. In any case, whether the music is slow (and the steps are like a wedding march) or fast (with more lively footwork), spacing and positioning are important during the entrance as well as throughout the piece.

The dance or movement choreography is typically very simple in a processional and there is more emphasis placed on the patterns and movement ideas. The following pages depict a few of the countless pattern ideas that can be done to make your processionals come alive. Please, take the basics from here and add, subtract, multiply, or divide any way that will make your movement equation balance to minister most effectively.

Crossing

Entire line cross each other (go from one ling to two) or try weaving in and out

Crossing on the diagonal or maybe make an X (takes more practice)

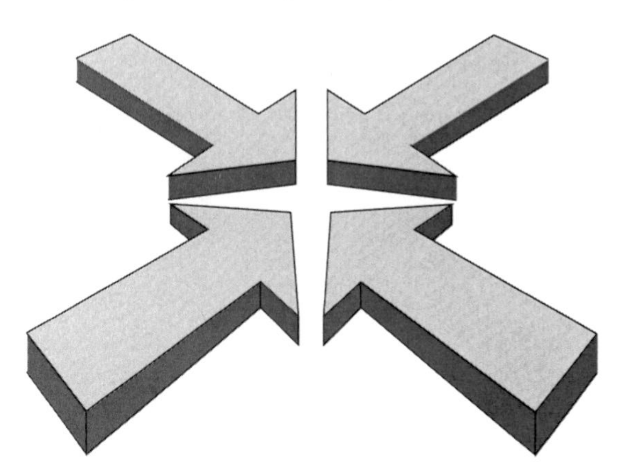

Crossing

One, two, or three at a time from corners

cross to make a cross

Circling

one large circle

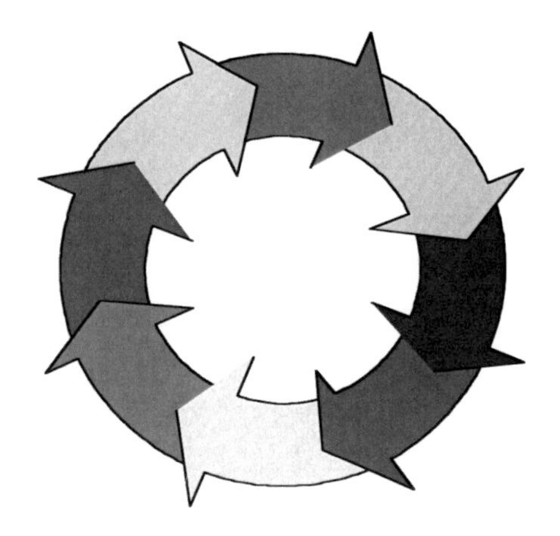

A Circle within a circle—either all going in the same direction or opposite

Circling

Two or more circles going in same or different directions

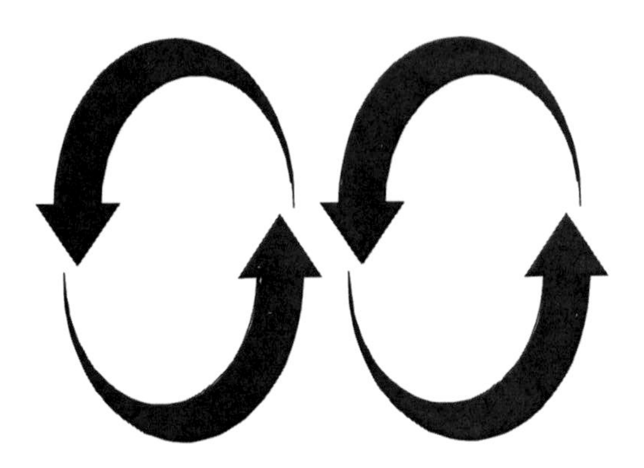

A circle within a circle—either all going in the same direction or opposite

Trading

Front line trades with back line—front line either turn around or walk backward

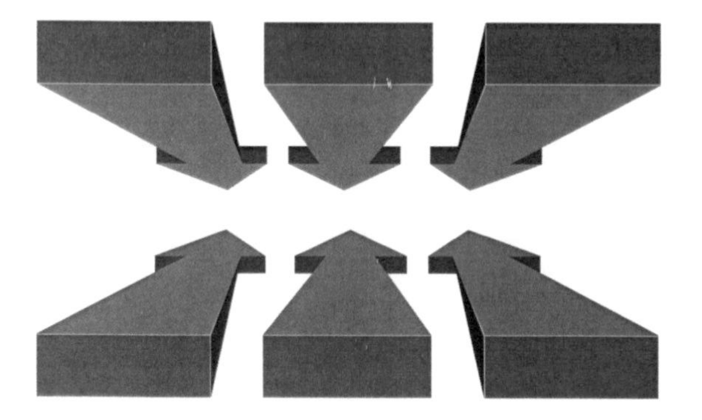

Coming from intermittent positioning, and making semi-circular trades. This creates a more interesting effect then simple front/ back trade

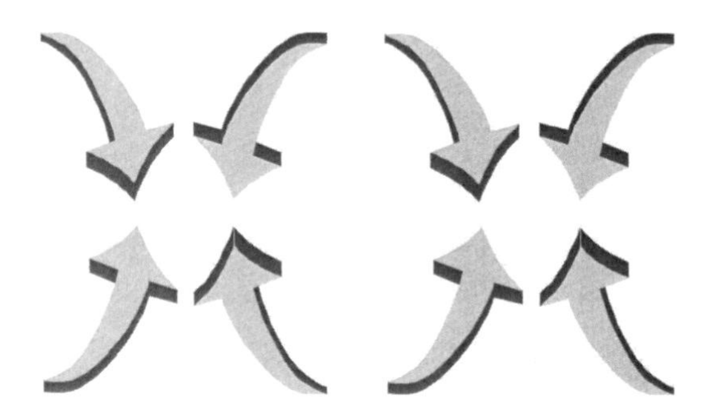

Trading

Lines or individuals trade sides vertically (provided there is enough room)

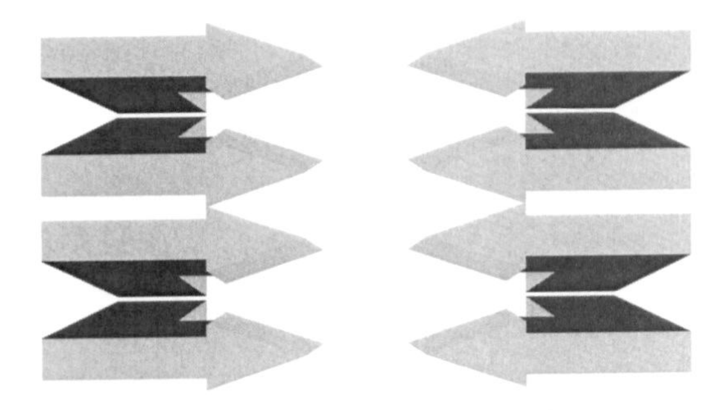

Person on inside end goes to opposite end of opposite line while everyone else moves down—can be done easier with straight lines, but may be interesting with a curve (maybe at the curve point, add a turn or gesture)

Peeling

Two or three rows approach each other—peel off in the middle in different directions—third line (in center) can cross each other to make two new lines

The hurricane effect—good transition move

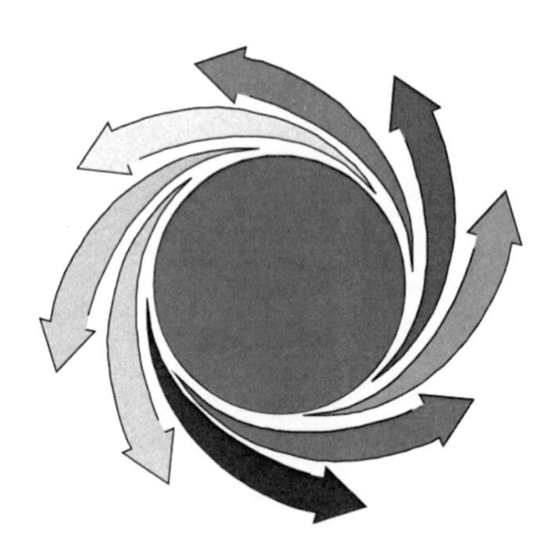

Peeling

A good way to move from front line to back line or exit down center isle

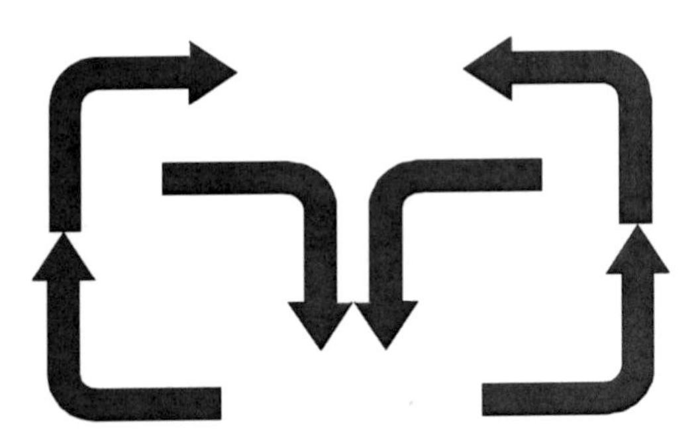

Good way to enter. Center arrow indicates forward motion—two lines side by side, peel off at front of sanctuary to create either one or two lines.

More Circles

Merge 4 people at a time from the diagonals and exit to the front/back/sides—since the exit is different from the entrance, 4 new people may enter the traffic circle—continue process.

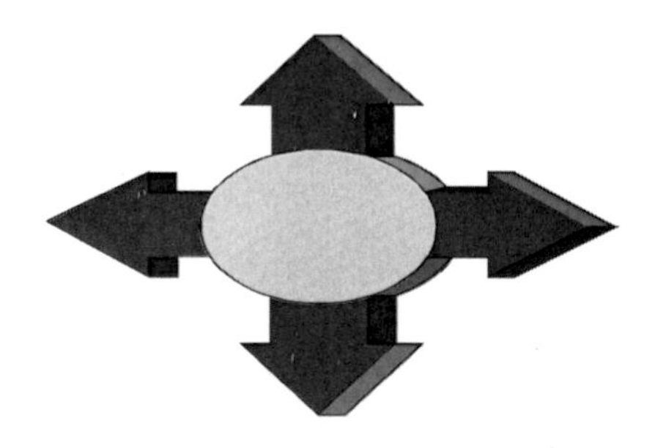

Rotate in the traffic circle—disperse into a front line.

More Circles

Either individuals or small groups come in from either sides or diagonals, do circular movements, then exit like traffic circle.

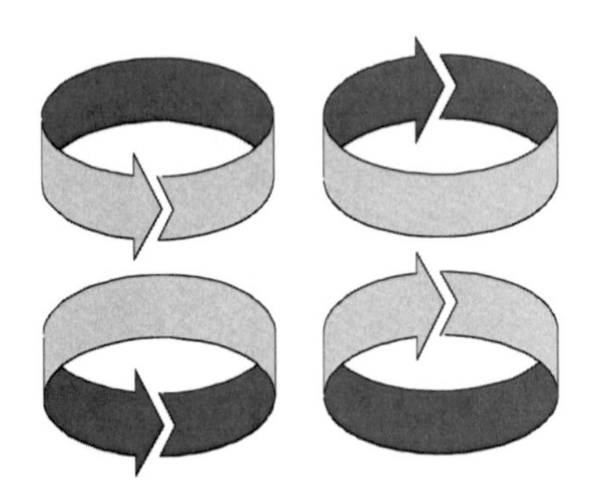

Orbit

individuals (or small groups of 2-3 each) revolve around a central person, group of people, or object while rotating in their own circle.

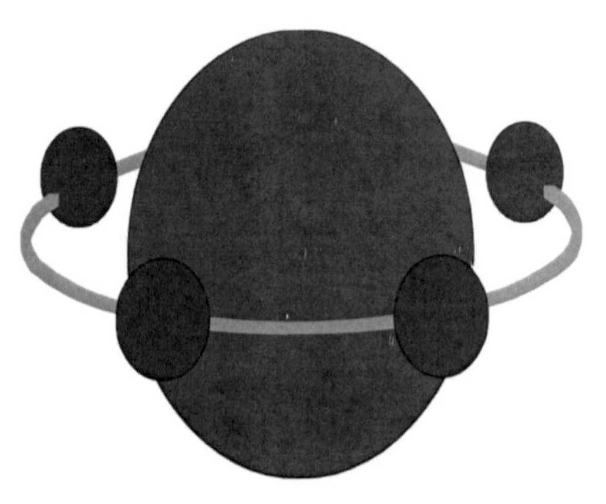

Other Designs

Rotate in military style (pivot at corners)

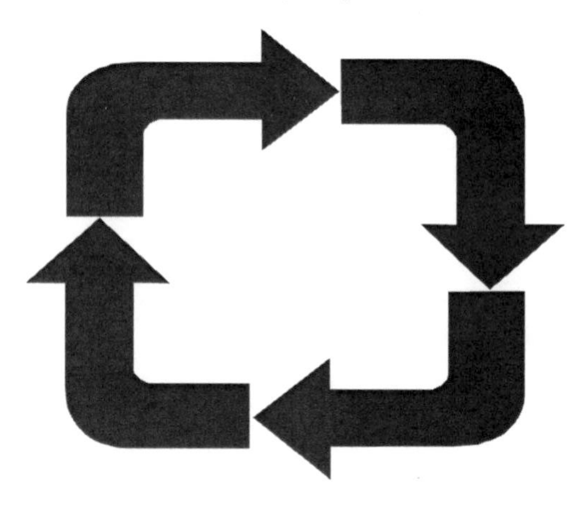

Have long row(s) or line(s) of people and short row(s) cross each other in middle, then whole grouping rotate—could hold hands/shoulders/waists or use props

Other Designs

move or do movements in triangular shape

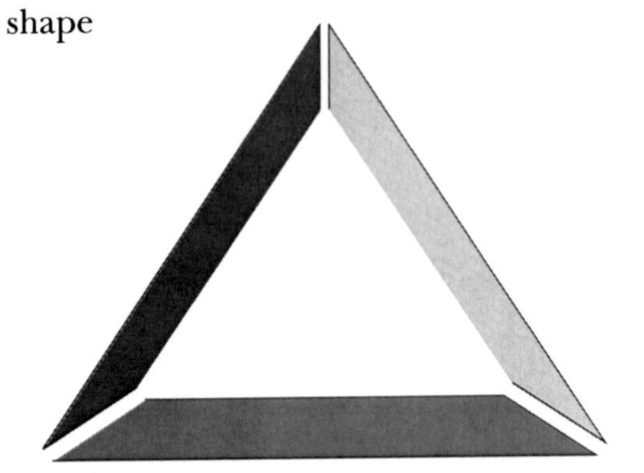

Have people 2x2 or 3x3 weave in zig zag pattern

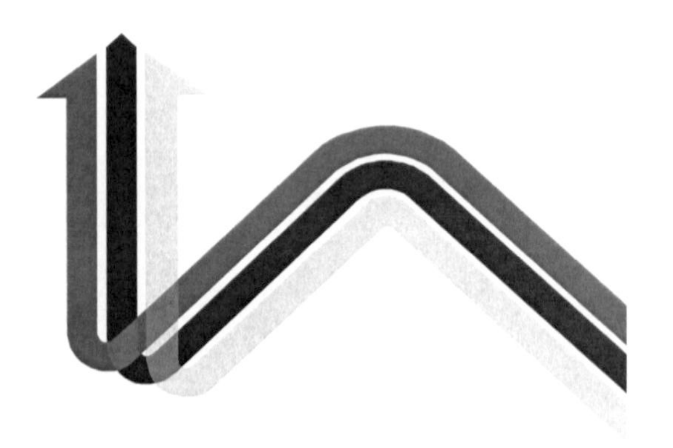

Part two: Props

Scriptural Significance

Practical Guide

John 12:12,13 – The next day a great multitude had come to the feast, when they heard that Jesus was coming to Jerusalem, Vs. 13 took branches of palm trees and went out to meet Him, and cried out: "Hosanna! Blessed is He who comes in the name of the Lord! The King of Israel!"

The great multitude waved palm fronds as a symbol of honor to Jesus. There are many instances in scripture where different items are in people's hands. Whether we wave palm branches or flags, it is helpful to understand the reason we wave. These next few chapters talk about props: their significance and practicality.

Scriptural Significance

Chapter 5: What's in the hand is worth…a lot

Revelation 7:9,10 – After these things I looked, and behold, a great multitude which no one could number, of all nations, tribes, peoples, and tongues, standing before the throne and before the Lamb, clothed with white robes, with palm branches in their hands, Vs. 10 and crying out with a loud voice, saying, "Salvation belongs to our God who sits on the throne, and to the Lamb!"

The vision was: of all the righteous redeemed who stood before the Lamb of God, waving their victory palm branches, while giving laudation and adulation to Him who sits upon the throne.

In this case having something in their hand signified victory and praise. The mention of these things has some kind of significance. Just like "one in the hand is worth two in the bush," *what is in the hand is worth a lot!* In other words, God would not mention various tools if they did not mean something. They had a purpose. These next few pages list some examples, seen throughout the bible, of worthwhile objects that were in people's hands.

These could serve as a reminder: when we praise the Lord with something in our hand (a flag, streamer, or whatever He tells us) it has some kind of significance.

KING'S SCEPTER

Esther 4:11 – "All the king's servants and the people of the king's provinces know that any man or woman who goes into the inner court to the king, who has not been called, he has but one law; put all to death, except the one to whom the king holds out the golden scepter, that he may live. Yet I myself have not been called to go in to the king these thirty days."

Esther 5:2 – So it was, when the king saw Queen Esther standing in the court, that she found favor in his sight, and the king held out to Esther the golden scepter that was in his hand. Then Esther went near and touched the top of the scepter.

The extension of a scepter was (as an emblem of one in authority) a symbolic representation of acceptance, grace (favor), entrance into the inner court of the king, and, in this case, preservation of life.

SHOFAR

Joshua 6:5– "It shall come to pass, when they make a long blast with the ram's horn (shofar), and when you hear the sound of the trumpet, that all the people shall shout with a great shout; then the wall of the city will fall down flat. And the people shall go up every man straight before him."

The process of walking proved their obedience and faith, while the resultant use of the instrumental implement proved the power of praise.

2 Samuel 2:28
Psalm 150:3
Exodus 19:13
Leviticus 25:9

TAMBOURINES (BRANDISHING BANNERS)

Is.30:32 – And in every place where the staff of punishment passes, which the Lord lays on him, it will be with tambourines (tabrets) and harps: and in battles of brandishing (shaking) will he fight with it.

Ephesians 2:1,2 – And you He made alive, who were dead in trespasses and sins, Vs. 2 in which you once walked according to the course of this world, according to the prince of the power of the air, the spirit who now works in the sons of disobedience.

Ephesians 6:12 – For we do not wrestle against flesh and blood, but against principalities, against powers, against the rulers of the darkness of this age, against spiritual hosts of wickedness in the heavenly places.

We know that we do not wrestle against flesh and blood, but against principalities etc. However, it is interesting to note that the use of tambourines does battle against the enemy!

TORCHES AND PITCHERS

Judges 7:20 – Then the three companies blew the trumpets and broke the pitchers – they held the torches in their left hands and the trumpets in their right hands for blowing – and they cried, "The sword of the Lord and of Gideon!"

This caused confusion in the enemy's camp, leading to ultimate victory for Gideon and his men.

MOSES' STAFF OR ROD

Exodus 7:20 – And Moses and Aaron did so, just as the Lord commanded. So he lifted up the rod and struck the waters that were in the river, in the sight of Pharaoh and in the sight of his servants. And all the waters that were in the river were turned to blood.

Psalm 23:4 – Yea, though I walk through the valley of death, I will fear no evil; for You are with me; Your rod and Your staff, they comfort me.

When going through sorrow, regret, repentance, and grief, it is often accompanied by and causes groaning of deep emotion, sighs and weeping. It is during these times, that the Lord, our shepherd, is ever present, experiencing and expressing not surface sympathy, but heart felt, absorbed, empathy and comfort.

Judges 6:21
Exodus 17:8-15

JAW BONE OF A DONKEY

Judges 15:16 – Then Samson said: "with the jawbone of a donkey, heaps upon heaps, with the jawbone of a donkey I have slain a thousand men!"

When it came time to do battle against the enemy, the Spirit of the Lord gave Samson supernatural strength with which to fight. Though he had broken one of his vows (by touching part of a dead animal), he was still able to use the fresh and strong (not dry and brittle) jawbone to gain great deliverance.

DAVID'S STONE AND SLING

I Samuel 17:49 – Then David put his hand in his bag and took out a stone; and he slung it and struck the Philistine in his forehead, so that the stone sank into his forehead, and he fell on his face to the earth.

This was the weapon of choice for David because he spent long hours practicing with it. It was the custom of that day to practice stone slinging until you became a good marksman. Nevertheless, God gave David the victory against a huge giant with His power exhibited in a little stone.

BREAD

Exodus 29:30 – "and you shall put all these in the hands of Aaron and in the hands of his sons, and you shall wave them as a wave offering before the Lord."

It was the law to offer many types of sacrifices to God. One, of which was the "wave offering." In doing so, many of the implements, animal parts, religious accouterment, etc. were lifted up and waved in order for it to be accepted by God. The following is just a small sample of things that were lifted as a wave offering for acceptable sacrifice:

FAT WITH BREAST OF AN ANIMAL

Leviticus 7:30
Leviticus 10:14

MALE LAMB AND LOG OF OIL

Leviticus 14:12

LAMB OF TRESPASS OFFERING AND LOG OF OIL

Leviticus 14:24

SHEAF OF THE FIRST FRUITS OF THE HARVEST

Leviticus 23:10-15

BOILED SHOULDER, ONE UNLEAVENED CAKE, AND ONE UNLEAVENED WAFER

Num. 6:19

Furthermore: The following definitions and root word notations may shed some insightful light on the subject of waving.

WAVE OFFERING—Tnuwphah (ten-oo-faw)—A perfume of fire that drives out the occupant (enemy). This is comparable to Qatar (that we saw in the processional section). Similarly, sweet incense to God (Nicowach) means restful delight. A brandishing (threat); by implication, tumult; specifically the official undulation of sacrificial offerings—offering, shaking, wave (offering).[1]

Root word—nuwph (noof)—a primitive root; to quiver (i.e. vibrate up and down, or rock to and fro); lift up, move, offer, perfume, send, shake, sift, strike, wave.[1]

Therefore, when we praise the Lord by waving our hands (with or without a loaf of bread or boiled shoulder) we can activate peace and rest in our lives because we are literally driving out the enemy of our soul. Since it is his job to steal, kill, and destroy anything that is, has, or gives life, then it is our job to foil those plans with the foe-defeating power of the Holy Spirit. Giving birth to Spirit-inspired dances and implement-handled movements is a catalyst that can execute a sweet smelling savor wave that drives out the occupant, causing deliverance. The remaining fruit is salvation, life, rest, and peace to the demonstrative "praiser," and in many cases, the quiescent on-looker.

Scriptural Significance

Chapter 6: His Banner

Zechariah 9:16-17- The Lord their God will save them in that day, as the flock of His people. For they shall be like the jewels of a crown, lifted like a banner over His land – Vs. 17 For how great is its (His) goodness and how great its (His) beauty!"

Jewels in a crown, waved as a banner, are a beautiful description of God's people. There are so many times the Word mentions banners or flags. In this chapter, I first wrote some of the definitions for flags and banners. Then I classified some of the scriptures according to their usage.

So often, we see banners and flags used in the church during praise and worship and presentations. It is good to have some scriptural understanding for use justification. I trust this compilation of biblical substantiation helps.

DEFINITIONS

BANNER nacac (naw-sas') "To gleam from afar; to be conspicuous as a signal; to raise a beacon; lift up as an ensign." [1]

BANNER: "A flag, ensign, streamer, or emblem attached to the end of a standard. Banners served as rallying points for military, national or religious purposes. Any figure or object (flag or banner) used as an emblem or symbol of a leader or people, military unit, or ensign of war. A piece of cloth bearing a design, motto, slogan, etc. Sometimes attached to a staff and used as a battle standard." [3]

FLAG "A piece of cloth or bunting varying in size, color, and design, used as a symbol, standard, signal, or emblem (Star spangled banner); To signal, give notice, or communicate with or as if with a flag; A headline extending across a newspaper page; A long strip of cloth with an advertisement, greeting etc. lettered on it." [3]

ENSIGN "A national flag displayed on ships and aircraft, often with the special insignia of a branch or unit of the armed forces; a band of colors; Any standard or banner, as of a military unit." [4]

STANDARD "A flag, banner, or ensign, specifically: The ensign of a chief of state, nation, or city, person or corporation; The colors of a motorized military unit; A pedestal, stand, or base." [3]

SIGNAL/COMMUNICATION/ PROCLAMATION

Is. 5:26 – He will lift up a banner to nations from afar, and will whistle to them from the end of the earth; surely they shall come with speed, swiftly.

The most common use of banners was for military campaigns. A large flag usually was raised on a hill or other high, visible place. It served as a signal for the war trumpets to be blown. In this case, God's judgement on Israel and Judah was set into action by calling on a foreign nation to bring retribution.

Banners declared communication and signaled or attracted attention so people could get involved in what ever was to take place next. Like a catalyst for drawing people together for orders, plans, news or action.

It is kind of like a 'tell-tail' on a sailing vessel. A tell-tail is a piece of yarn that is tied to the metal wires ('stays' that hold up the mast) way up high for all to see. When the wind blows the tell-tail, the tail tells the captain from which way the wind is blowing. Once he knows this, he can maneuver the boat and trim the sails to accomplish the best point of sail. This will make the boat go at the best rate of speed in the best direction. If you were racing, this small piece of yarn could be instrumental in helping you win the race.

During a church service, if someone in leadership is very much tuned into the "wind of the Spirit', they may do something to declare communication. For example, they could suggest that someone walk across the front of the sanctuary with a banner that says, "The River Is Here." This one action may change the whole format, feel and direction of the service toward the best "point of sail" or "time of ministry." It may declare communication for new orders from the Holy Spirit.

Jeremiah 50:2 – "Declare among the nations, proclaim, and set up a standard; proclaim – do not conceal it – say, Babylon is taken, Bel is shamed. Merodach is broken in pieces; Her idols are humiliated, her images are broken in pieces."

Another function of banners is proclamation or prophetic declaration. In this case, it is of what will happen to Babylon when the people rally together under the banner.

Jeremiah 51:27 – Set up a banner in the land, blow the trumpet among the nations! Prepare the nations against her, call the kingdoms together against her: Ararat, Minni, and Ashkenaz. Appoint a general against her; cause the horses to come like the bristling locusts.

This is another summons against Babylon signifying unity among the soldiers during a common cause and time for strategy.

Isaiah 18:3 – All inhabitants of the world and dwellers on the earth: When he lifts up a banner on the mountains, you see it; and when he blows a trumpet, you hear it.

When God lifts up a banner, everyone sees it.

Isaiah 13:2-3 – Lift up a banner on the high mountain, raise your voice to them; wave your hand, that they may enter the gates of the nobles. Vs 3 I have commanded My sanctified ones; I have also called My mighty ones for My anger – Those who rejoice in My exaltation."

God set apart a special task force against this particular group of people (kind of like Top Gun Navy pilots). The on-looking Israel "cheers them on" (probably from on a hill) as they go by (like rooting for your favorite team while sitting high in the bleachers). A banner indicates that soldiers can come together in a spirit of unity for one cause, under one banner. The flag becomes an object of hope in the midst of a battle.

IDENTIFICATION

Numbers 1:52 – The children of Israel shall pitch their tents, everyone by his own camp, everyone by his own standard, according to their armies.

Numbers 2:34 – Thus the children of Israel did according to all that the Lord commanded Moses; so they camped by their standards and so they broke camp, each one by his family, according to their fathers' houses.

Numbers 2:2-3 – Everyone of the children of Israel shall camp by his own standard.

"Four large, banner-bearing standards (one on each of the four sides of the tabernacle of meeting) were used by the 12 tribes of Israel during their wilderness journeys." [2]

This use of the word banner refers specifically to the military cohort's camp, which is a company of soldiers or military assemblage of 300-600 men. It also lets people know with whom you identify (king, colors, kingdom, characteristics, etc.).

Jeremiah 4:5-6 – Declare in Judah and proclaim in Jerusalem, and say: "Blow the trumpet in the land; Cry, gather together, and say assemble yourselves, and let us go into the fortified cities. Vs. 6 Set up the standard (banner) toward Zion. Take refuge! Do not delay! For I will bring disaster from the north, and great destruction."

Jeremiah 4:21 - How long will I see the standard (banner) and hear the sound of the trumpet?

A flag on a pole signaled danger and a place for assembly. This is the type, model, or example to which there is general acceptance or adherence.

Soldiers always carried their identifying flag with them into battle, so if someone got off on their own, or got lost, they could look up and see their banner of safety. They could then re-set their course appropriately.

The Lord our Banner represents hope and safety in the midst of personal battles.

WARFARE/VICTORY IN BATTLE

Ps. 20:4-5 – May He grant you according to your heart's desire, and fulfill all your purpose. Vs. 5 We will rejoice in your salvation and in the name of our God we will set up our banners! May the Lord fulfill all your petitions.

They set up banners in the name of God during a time of intercession for the ones going to war. It was like a prophetic proclamation of triumph and a trophy in His honor. This type of demonstrative proclamation is conspicuous and flaunts victory in the enemy's face. They waved banners to Celebrate victory won and answered prayers!

Isaiah 59:19 - So shall they fear the name of the Lord form the West, and His glory from the rising of the sun. When the enemy comes in like a flood, the Spirit of the Lord will lift up a standard against him.

We are certain that the enemy of our soul will come into close contact with the invincible and overpowering

Spirit of the Living God. A presentation of a banner can literally cause the enemy to flee because the Spirit of the Lord is the one who lifts up a standard against him. It invades the air space of the prince of the power of the air, and destroys him.

JESUS/TRUTH

Ps. 60:4 – You have given a banner to those who fear You, that it may be displayed because of the truth. Vs. 5 That Your beloved may be delivered, save with Your right hand, and hear me.

"The banner was a rallying point for the defense of the truth that Israel possessed in the midst of a pagan world of ignorance." [2]

Banners with words or scriptures (Majesty, King of Kings, etc.) give honor where honor is due and display God's Truth. *"You shall know the truth, and the Truth shall make you free."* The word of God on a banner as well as use of the representative colors can be an effective ministry tool.

Isaiah 11:10 – "And in that day there shall be a Root of Jesse, who shall stand as a banner to the people; for the gentiles shall seek Him, and His resting place shall be glorious."

John 12:32 – "And I, if I am lifted (crucified) up from the earth, will draw all peoples to Myself"

Lifting Jesus (like a redemptive streamer or gathering place for healing) on the cross (standard) demonstrates God's presence in the midst of His people. This sign (ensign) of Truth, visible from all around, directed His people to salvation and God's will.

John 3:14-16 – And as Moses lifted up the serpent in the wilderness (Num. 21:8-9) even so must the Son of Man be lifted up, Vs. 15 that whoever believes in Him should not perish but have eternal life. Vs. 16 For God so loved the world that He gave His only begotten son, that whoever believes in Him should not perish but have everlasting life.

After repentance from their sin of murmuring and complaining against the Lord, they begged Moses to do something. Moses then prayed and God instructed him to erect a pole with a fiery serpent on it. God also instructed the people to look to it (a type of Christ on the cross) in faith, be healed and live. The idea is not to look at the object to obtain healing, because that would be nothing but superstition and even lend itself to witchcraft. Looking to Jesus (the Lord God our healer) with faith believing, will bring healing and life. Likewise, when we carry flags, streamers, cloths, and even beautiful banners, it is not those articles of worship that perform the miracle, but is the almighty God who works through a vessel who is obedient to do His work.

PERSONAL/MODERN DAY/CHURCH

Psalm 74:4-5,8 – Your enemies roar in the midst of Your meeting place; they set up their banners for signs. Vs. 5 They seem like men who lift up axes among the thick trees Vs. 8 They said in their hearts, "Let us destroy them altogether."

The enemy's camp has standards too. He will attempt to destroy the lives of the congregation right in the middle of the meeting place (the church). This is even more reasoning to wave banners in defiance of his tactics and for the defeat of his camp.

Song of Solomon 6:10 – Who is she who looks forth as the morning, fair as the moon, clear as the sun, awesome as an army with banners?

What type of banners do we wave? Do our lives reflect the character of Christ as clearly as the moon reflects the sun? Do our lives honestly depicted banners we bear or portray symbolism of the flags we wave? What is our attitude? Do we project clarity of innocence and purity of heart as we dance or wave our banners? God is molding us to be as awesome as an army with banners.

Song of Solomon 2:4 – He brought me to the banqueting house, and his banner over me was love.

This shows God's protection and covering of love.

BECOMING A LIVING BANNER

Exodus 17:15 – And Moses built an alter and called its name The Lord our Banner (Jehovah Nissi).

When the Israelites fought the Amelekites, at Raphidium, Moses held up his hand, thus becoming a living banner, symbolizing God's presence to help his people win the victory.

When we rely on God (the Lord our banner) and surrender to Him (our victor), we will win the battle against the flesh. As long as we raise His banner, and keep it up (as Moses did), we have victory over our circumstances.

Likewise, when we hold up the arms of our leaders and other team members, it will help them get through whatever enemy-induced battle they may be going. Encouragement like that offers them hope and support. Ultimately, it aids in their victory.

Isaiah 62:10 – Go through, go on through the gates, clear the way for the people! Build up a highway, build it up. Clear away the stones. Raise a Banner for the peoples.

In earlier verses, the Lord swore by His right hand that He would not give the food and new wine (for which there had been much labor) to the enemies; but would allow the harvesters to eat and drink of it in His holy courts. After they followed the directions given by the Lord, He then commanded them to prepare the way for the people, one example of which was to lift up banners for them.

We can see the significant and prolific use of banners throughout the Word. Should it not stand to reason that we be able to use flags and banners as part of our worship to the Lord and as warfare against the enemy? Should we not be able to disturb the airways against the principalities to gain victory for our God? Let us then lift His banner high over our circumstances and wave!

Practical Guide

Chapter 7: Prop Incorporation

I Samuel 17:40 – Then he took his staff in his hand; and he chose for himself five smooth stones from the brook, and put them in a shepherd's bag, in a pouch which he had, and his sling was in his hand. And he drew near to the Philistine.

They initially outfitted David with inappropriate battle array. He needed the right weapon, at the right time, for the right task because he had a purpose and goal in mind that no sword or other weapon could accomplish. Wisdom won, as he chose the stones and sling, because *incorporation* of that appropriate "prop" was sure to help him be victorious!

Just as David had the right prop to win a battle, so can worship dancers incorporate the use of a suitable prop as an aid to clearly convey a life-changing message. Although the name of the chapter sounds like a business title, we are not going to launch a company called "Props Inc.." I simply want to talk about incorporating the use of appropriate props for presentations. Almost all dramas or plays are done with props. They could range anywhere from a huge scenery backdrop to a small feather pen. Everything on the stage has a purpose for being there. If the actors do not specifically use the prop, it may be there simply to create an atmosphere, era, or theme. If nothing else, it could be there for eye-appealing décor. Likewise, when we use any of a wide variety of props in drama dances (or fondly known as "dramances"), they should have some kind of purpose or function. They should give or create messages that are 'audience friendly' (the audience should be able to understand what message you are trying to convey with their use). They should also be executed with good over-all design and be well rehearsed if they are used for movement embellishment, visual effect, or musical interpretation.

Just as we saw in the previous chapters, how the Bible mentions the use of numerous and varied objects for various purposes, so can the worship dancer use countless types of props. Since you already have a scriptural foundation for props and flags, and will have an understanding of color in a later chapter, the possibilities are endless! There is much freedom in having this knowledge. Be creative!

The following are some widely used common props. However, with greater understanding, the sky is the limit for what type of implements you can create. Almost all of these can be hand made. With a little ingenuity and access to the local craft and fabric stores, you can produce fabulous creations at minimal cost.

BANNERS

There are several connotations of the word banner. They could be: flags, ensigns, small hoops (hand banners) and even tambourines. However, I am going to refer to banners as those exquisite, large, four to six - foot length cloths that usually demonstrate a message of truth, and are displayed on a long pole (usually in a procession). Here are just a couple tips about banners:

As I mentioned in Chapter 4, the banners can be better viewed if they enter from the side aisles and turn inward (toward the congregation). The banner bearer should place the pole on the inside hip (the one closest to the congregation). He should hold the lower portion of the pole with the outside hand (for support), and the upper portion of the pole with the inside hand (for balance and maneuverability). Then, that person should easily be able to display that banner of Truth. Just a side note here: Banners of this magnitude, splendor and beauty should be handled with utmost respect, care and grace. Never shake the banners up and down, no matter how badly you want to keep up with the increased tempo of the music. It is extremely distracting and does not minister. For the best effect, the banner bearer should move throughout the sanctuary more slowly then what seems normal. If the banners are stationed, momentarily at the front of the sanctuary (with all eyes upon it) it may be waved, ever so slowly in a forward and backward movement. This may be easily done with the hand and pole positioning that I mentioned earlier. Holsters are available through parade supply places. Often, the sequins and glitter will reflect the spotlights, sending off resplendent beams of radiant light!

FLAGS

There are numerous types of flags. Some may be purchased through catalogues, while others may be hand crafted. The most simply constructed are material glued on a dowel. We started with these in our church. Simply acquire small wooden dowels from a local craft store. Purchase some lame' or silk-type material. Glue an end of the cut square of material to the pole. Voila, flag! The size of the flag depends on the size of the pole and material. It is up to you. Although, there are more elaborate ways to make them, this is a good start.

STREAMERS

Streamers can be as large or as small as you want or can handle. You can make finger streamers with little plastic rings (found in a craft store) and ribbon, or huge banner-like ones that can write God's signature in the sky! With a little creativity, these can also be hand made. Get a dowel, fishing tackle that swivels, and 'flowy' material of your choice (be careful that the material is not too heavy). They can be made more elaborately adding grommets, and string, etc. Use your ingenuity.

TAMBOURINES

Tambourines may be purchased at a music store where they sell instruments. They are often in Christian bookstores as well. The type is up to you. There are the kind with the skin in the middle (good for praise and worship dancing) or the musical kind with no middle. To either kind, you may add ribbons, or tinsel-type streamers that create an interesting effect when swirled over head. There is actually a whole movement vocabulary associated with them.

LAURELS

These are Mylar or flower covered embroidery hoops. They add a nice touch to a processional or dance.

ARCHES

Arches can be made from hula-hoops. Simply cut one in half and glue (or securely tie) silk flowers, or Mylar pieces. They are wonderful for weddings or processionals where people go under them (one person standing on each side of the aisle, holding one end of the arch). They are also great for one person to hold an end in each hand while they process with several others doing the same thing. Patterns can then be created with them like back-back rotating in a circle; pinwheel type effect; stand in a line and do 'the wave'; switch places while holding them up; the possibilities are endless.

SILK ESSENCE OR LAME' CLOTHS

Lame' billows more easily then silk and is usually on sale around Christmas time. Silks come in a broader variety of colors and may be used effectively for interpretation. Five yards is a good length to billow, and it is a good idea to hem the non-selvage edges. You can do more then just billow cloths. You can: billow then come together in the middle; trade places with your partner; turn it sideways and whoosh it forward and back; two cloths can make an X or cross; you can billow up and have the top cloth people cross each other under the bottom cloth; after you have crossed, you can turn them sideways and make a pinwheel while walking in a circle. These and other things can be done with more then two cloths. Have fun experimenting!

HOOPS

Like laurels, hoops can be made from embroidery hoops and ribbon or Mylar tinsel. This type of tinsel is more readily available around Christmas and can be found at most discount department stores. However, you can really let your creative imagination run wild at a craft store and a trip to a party store is always fun.

Almost all the dances that I choreographed have been somewhat "interpretive." That means that the dancer(s) give meaning to the words of the song through dramatic movements. Expressive sign language, dramatic movement gestures, the use of props, or any combination thereof can accomplish this. An interpretive dance should portray a relatively clear message to the audience. They should be able to grasp or understand your interpretation of the main theme of the song, at least. When you incorporate a prop, careful forethought should go into its selection. If a sailor on a ship was to motion to another with his signal flags, and he was not careful, catastrophe could occur. One false flag and his message might state something inappropriate like "happy Valentines Day," when what he needed or meant to say was "an enemy destroyer ship is coming!"

With message clarity and interpretation in mind, I would like to share a small sampling of how I incorporated and have seen others incorporate props into dances or presentations.

In the dance "What Sin," I used a five yard, *blue* silk essence cloth to represent the sea of forgetfulness. At the end of the dance, the three dancers that represented torment and sin, were buried in the sea of forgetfulness.

They crouched down on their knees and the cloth covered them entirely.

In the dance "Yahweh," we had 4 huge (about 2 ½ feet in diameter) gold worship hoops that represented the glory and goodness of God. Two ladies held the hoops over their heads and walked on the floor (in front of the stage) from one side of the sanctuary to the other, passing in front of the dancers who were on the stage. As they passed, the dancers reacted by covering their eyes (so as not to see the face of God nor the intensity of His resplendent glorious presence). In the song, when the singer proclaimed "Let your goodness pass before us, right before our eyes," there was no mistaking what those hoops represented. There was also a tangible sense of God's presence as it went by.

When we did "I See The Lord," we used a five-yard gold lame' cloth to represent His train filling the temple. They processed to the stage from the back of the church, down the center aisle, with the cloth held way above their heads (one person holding up each end). After making their way to the front, while the verse repeated, a second "train" of like kind came down the aisle, adding more impact. 'His hair was white as snow' was represented by a white five-yard Pearl Essence cloth. Finally, an angel 'touched the coal to "Isaiah's" lips' with a set of fireplace tongs.

When we did "Dancing Before You" (a song depicting Revelation 4), we erected a throne to represent—you guessed it—a throne! Streaming from and attached to the throne, however, were (one end each of) four five-yard silk essence cloths. Gold represented the throne and God's glory. Green represented the emerald or rainbow. Red represented the sardius stone, and white represented the jasper stone. As the designated words were mentioned, each dancer (who was holding one end of a certain cloth) would billow it up in the air accordingly. Since that particular color cloth was the only thing moving during that part of the song, it was obvious what the interpretation was. If, on the other hand, we had used those same cloths in another dance, without the word interpretation but with the same color understanding, the audience may not catch it. They may say, "Oh what lovely cloths, I wonder why they are waving them."

This is what I mean about a clear message. You do not want to leave the audience wondering too much. The use of props should not be ambiguous, but have application; should not be a distraction, but be demonstratively descriptive; and should not be obscure, but illustratively illuminate!

Many years ago, I did a dance that was interpretive and understandable, or so I thought. At the time, I did not have much in the way of props or costumes, so I thought it would be fitting to use what I did have. The teal colored sash in my hand, which I waved gracefully throughout the dance, looked pretty and "most important," matched my outfit. Unfortunately, it did not make any sense at all to the curious on-lookers. The only reason I know that I left the audience scrambling for an explanation (about this mysterious cloth), was that one brave soul came up to me afterward and asked about it. With utmost sincerity and I am sure after much mental deliberation, he asked me what kind of deep spiritual meaning was behind the green cloth.

Somewhat embarrassed that I did not have a revelatory eschatological explanation and knowing that the cloth was not at all a necessary element for interpretation, I blurted the truth: "it matched my skirt." After observing the perplexed look and minor disappointment on his face, I learned my lesson. From then on, I tried to use props that had some kind of purpose or function.

This is not to say that dances should only incorporate props with deep, specific, spiritual meaning. Again, we understand the underlying scriptural justification for the use of flags or props in general, (as we learned in the previous chapter). Nevertheless, if they do not have *specific* interpretation or scriptural significance, then their purpose or function may be to augment a dance with visual appeal or artistic design. I have done and seen many dances that use props for visual effect. They add dimensional design, fullness, and excitement.

The point is that even if the prop use is for embellishment, let us say, then **that** is its purpose or function. For example there is a song called "Stir It Up" to which dancers utilize small hand-banners (multi-colored, Mylar-fringed, oval-shaped hoops– about ten inches across and six inches wide). When the singers sing "stir it up," the dancers commence stirring. The Mylar "fringie" does not *mean* stir. The colors in the "fringie" do not *represent* the word stir. Without question, we know that using any kind of banner or flag at any time during praise and worship or a presentation wreaks havoc on the enemy so that purpose is always evident. However, in addition to the obvious warfare aspect of "fringie" use, it is in this case, simply an extension of the dancers' hands, making the movements easier to see and more clearly defined.

Streamers can be used in a variety of ways. I saw a dance done to "Ancient of Days" where in addition to wonderful overall choreography, the dancers used props to specifically interpret the music. This was the long version with a musical interlude in the middle of the song. When the bass guitar played, the dancers kept time (with very simple movements) in the back of the stage with laurels. Then, when the flute played, one of the dancers swiftly, twirled a long streamer as she did a rapid, delicate movement across the stage. It awakened our senses and we, as an audience, were awed by the delightful interpretation .

Whether the purpose is to portray scriptural significance with message clarity, embellish expressive movement, have dramatic visual effect and design, or specifically interpret music, it is important to choose props appropriately.

Practical Guide

Chapter 8: Mishap or happy

Psalm 30:4-5 – Sing praise to the Lord, you saints of His, and give thanks at the remembrance of His holy name. Vs.5 For His anger is but for a moment, ***His favor is for life;*** *weeping may endure for a night,* ***but joy comes in the morning.***

His favor is for life, and joy comes in the morning. These certainly are comforting words to hear when you have just made a mistake during a presentation or praise and worship. I used to think, years ago, that because we prayed before a dance, that there would not be any mishaps or mistakes. I have since discovered that even the most powerful prayers can not stop the occasional inevitable. Fortunately, the anointing does cover a multitude of ***mishaps***, the people soon forget, and as long as we do not let our faces show it, we and the audience will be ***happy***. In this chapter, not only would I like to share some of the mishaps that have happened during praise and worship and presentations pieces, but also some basic tips on how to avoid them.

We have all had embarrassing moments in our lives, none of which we like. However, with a good attitude and a merry heart, we can soon look back and laugh. The use of props in presentation pieces or during praise and worship adds a dimension of difficulty that requires extra practice. There is also an increased chance of mishap. Be encouraged. Many people have and will have experienced the same thing. Sometimes, no matter how much you practice or examine the possibilities, things just happen.

One of the first times I used a five-yard cloth, I got all tangled up! During the Feast of Tabernacles, in front of a packed-house audience, four of us were holding the ends of two cloths. We had practiced the cross-under-trade places maneuver many times. For some reason, on this night, I either turned the wrong way, or went under in the wrong direction or something, because we had a knot in the middle that could definitely not be untied gracefully. We tried billowing up and going back to our original spots, but that only made matters worse. We tried going back again, and then it was really bad. We smiled and pretended like nothing was wrong while our eyes were shooting 'what do we do now?!' signals from across the cloth. Finally, we concluded that the only way out of this was to stop what we were doing and just untie the knot. Ungraceful, and humiliating as it was, that is what we did. There were a few moments of entire embarrassment, but like getting back up on a horse after having fallen off, we just picked up where we left off (as if nothing had ever happened). I am sure the forgiving audience soon forgot.

I will never forget one incident when we did a very reverent, very holy, worshipful dance using a pearl essence five-yard cloth. A couple of times during the song, two teens were to billow it up and trade places. This seemed simple enough and during practices, it always went without a hitch. Two of us were situated in front of the horizontally positioned cloth, and two were behind. During one of the crossings, I heard a gasp come from the audience. Out of my peripheral vision, I saw that my partner had been "clotheslined"! Fortunately, she remained composed enough to get out of it (as gracefully as one could under the circumstances) and completed the dance. She also never let her face show that there was a mishap. Again, for that moment, we were all concerned, but the audience was more compassionate then cynical.

Sometimes, props will come out of people's hands. I have seen a small baton flag fly. I have seen medium to large flags drop. What really makes you gasp is when you are holding the end of a billow cloth (especially when it is choreographed) and you accidentally let go of the corner. What's even worse is if you have both corners pulled right out of your hands and have to run forward to pick it up. Remember, do not feel badly if this has happened to you because it has happened to many others and as I said earlier, the audience is forgiving and compassionate. One preventative measure tip that may be helpful is to wrap the corner around your index finger and hold the remaining end *tightly* in your palm. This takes about six to eight inches from both ends and usually creates permanent wrinkles in the corners, but it is worth it in the long run. By the way, it is a good idea to put a zigzag hem on your lame' cloths so they don't fray.

Sometimes we use a small cloth (about four feet by five feet square). I can not tell you how many times I have stepped on it there by pulling it right out of my hand. No matter how determined I become (that this time I am not going to drop it) and no matter how tightly I hold on, occasionally, I still drop it and have to stop and pick it up.

Sometimes, it is better to leave the prop on the floor. When I taught "All Honor" at a workshop, one hundred and thirty people participated in the dance. It was massive and powerful! Each person had three very small cloths (white: Holy Spirit; yellow and red: fire). To make a long story short, during one segment of the dance, they were moving from one side of the huge auditorium to the other while simultaneously waving these cloths. Observing this flag-like fury, reminded me that when there is a large chorus of dancers, and you happen to drop one of your cloths, rather then impeding traffic, or causing a distraction, just leave it on the floor. It will probably go unnoticed. Contrary to our own bombarding thoughts, the audience is probably not focusing their attention on you as an individual. They are more then likely observing the presentation as a whole and a minor incident does not distract them.

Any time you try a new "special effect," you run the risk of flop. I had this brainstorm vision to try to have some kind of sequins billow up from the middle of a billow cloth. I was hoping that it would be propelled high up in the air and as it fluttered down (to the music: "Holy Spirit in graceful descent..."), the billow cloth would turn sideways and "blow" it out to the people in the congregation. Aside from this being a possible janitors nightmare, I also did not take into consideration the air-conditioning duct in the ceiling that might distort the billowing. Since I did not want to use up the sequins during practice, we did not practice with them. You can only imagine what happened. Nothing. The sequins were too heavy to fly any distance up. The cloths kind of went on an angle because of the air conditioning duct, the people in the middle and the back did not see them at all, and it was still a janitor's nightmare! Oh well. The lesson learned? Practice, practice, practice.

Well, practice does make perfect, but sometimes special effects need to be perfectly practiced. When we did "Creator of the Universe," we decided to add more impact to The Creator's entrance. I ventured out to the music store and rented a fog machine. My first clue that this may have been the wrong thing to do should have been that I was renting a fog machine that was usually used at rock concerts and bars. I just knew, though, that it would be an awesome effect to have God walk on the clouds. We had one chance to practice before the actual presentation and we squirted out a tiny bit of cloud (just to see if it worked). It worked well enough and everyone was thrilled. The day of the production, everything went very well and it came time for God's grand entrance. The prop department emitted the cloud on time. However, instead of God walking ***on*** it, He walked ***through*** a huge cloud of fog that consumed Him, the rest of the dancers, *and the entire congregation!* Oops! The morals of this story are take some advice from others (like the ones who said we should use dry ice instead) and practice (full out) the way it is supposed to be.

Sometimes the most precious and beautiful props can turn out to be a little costly and messy. We did a dance one time where we incorporated the children's dance team. As they went single file down the center isle, they had beautifully decorated baskets from which they scattered multi-colored rose petals on to the floor. The music that was playing in the background to this touching scene was "There will never be a name sweeter then the name of Jesus." The moms joyfully elbowed their husbands as they pointed to their precious children. The endearing sound of "Awwwwww" was heard throughout the sanctuary and we all were very pleased. By the end of service, however, after all two hundred or so people trampled on those petals on their way out, many mementos remained. The stains that were left behind were too numerous to count and too stubborn to scrub. The experts came, but to no avail. The next step…new carpet. They said they needed new carpet anyway and this was a good excuse as any to go ahead and make the purchase. All was forgiven and everything was fine. Never the less, and needless to say, we learned that any time we are going to use fresh flowers that will drop on the floor, that we will get one of those paper runners (like they use for weddings).

One Christmas, we did a processional, and why I felt compelled to practice *every single time* **with** the battery operated candles, I will never know. We only needed twelve candles, but started out with fourteen—just in case any might break. I was so happy the woman in charge of the props thought ahead for me. Since we had so many people in the dance, and it included six five-yard billow cloths, we had most of our practices in the gym. After the dancers were finished with their candle entrance, they were to put them on the floor and pick up their billow cloths. Shatter! Oops! One of the cloths had knocked a candle onto the cement floor. We paused to sweep the mess and all vowed to be more careful next time. Several practices went with out a hitch until—Crack! Oh no, not another one! We really had to be careful because, at that point, there were just enough candles for everyone. It was not until the dress rehearsal that we found out there were only ten working candles. I ended up putting two worshippers in the middle of the line with no candles. They simply raised their hands as they walked. It all worked out, but the mishaps could have been avoided had we just practiced one time with the candles in our hands (maybe even without the bulbs) and then put them away until the presentation. Live and learn.

Finally, if you are going to incorporate props in praise and worship or during a presentation, be sure to *be aware of what is around you.* Be aware of your space or lack thereof. Someone poked very near my eye with a flagpole, one time. I know others who also have gotten 'shiners' from well meaning worshippers. I have seen musicians play their instruments while having to 'duck' to avoid low flying streamers and flags. We have run into this problem many times. Should the person using the prop step aside, not use the prop all together, or watch out for the other guy? Or, should the other guy watch out for the prop, step aside, or not go near the prop all together? It is a matter of common sense and common courtesy. Be aware of your surroundings. Watch out for ceiling fans, low doorways, and chandeliers (particularly if you are carrying a large banner). One woman shared a story many years ago, about her minor (near) catastrophe. She had just been given permission to use flags during praise and worship and apparently, she had at least one very large one. Well, during praise and worship, she exuberantly began running up the isle, swinging the flag around over her head. Something she did not take into consideration was the beautiful chandelier that decorated the elegant sanctuary. You guessed it…CRASH! There must have been a protective angel 'swinging from the chandelier' that day because it miraculously did not break. Case in point…watch your surroundings!

IN SUMMARY:

- If you make a mistake, don't let your face show it.
- Pick up where you left off or just keep on going.Don't give up on the dance.
- Don't be a distraction if you experience "prop-drop." Either leave it on the floor or pick it up quickly and gracefully to continue your movements.
- Practice, practice, practice!!!
- Listen to good advice. There is wisdom in the counsel of many.
- Use protective measures for potential messes.
- Be acutely aware of your surroundings when using props.

Never become discouraged if you make a mistake or cause a mishap. It can happen to anyone. Keep in mind that although the problem seems glaring, it is minuscule compared to the many wonderful and successful prop presentations that you will have accomplished. You can turn your mishap into happiness with the right attitude and the comforting knowledge that...His favor is for life and...joy comes in the morning.

Part three: Pageantry

Scriptural Significance

Chapter 9—God loves color

Chapter 10—Faith in a material world

Practical Guide

Chapter 11—Creative Costuming
Chapter 12—Ministry Palette

I Chronicles 22:5– Now David said, "Solomon my son is young and inexperienced, and the house to be built for the Lord must be exceedingly magnificent, famous and glorious throughout all countries. I will now make preparation for it."

The definition of **magnificent** is: "great in splendor; lavish; grand or imposing to the mind; marked by nobility of thought or deed; exalted; outstanding of its kind; superlative."[4] It is interesting that not only was the house for the Lord to be magnificent, but it was to be *exceedingly* magnificent! How much more magnificent should our pageantry that we do *in* the house of the Lord be?

PAGEANT/PAGEANTRY "An elaborate public dramatic presentation, usually depicting some historical or traditional event; A spectacular procession or celebration; Colorful display; Showy display; pomp. Grand or flashy display." [4]

Scriptural Significance

Chapter 9: God loves color!

Psalm 27:4 – One thing I have desired of the Lord, that will I seek: that I may dwell in the house of the Lord all the days of my life, to behold the ***beauty*** *(delightfulness) of the Lord, and to inquire in His temple.*

Ps. 96:6 – Honor and majesty are before Him; strength and ***beauty*** *are in His sanctuary.*

Exodus 15:11 – "Who is like you, O Lord, among the gods? Who is like You, ***glorious*** *(festive, pleasant, admirable) in holiness, fearful in praises, doing wonders?*

The definition of beauty is: "A pleasing quality associated with harmony of form or **color**, excellence of craftsmanship, truthfulness, originality, or other, often unspecifiable property."[4]

According to this definition, and these scriptures, both the Lord and His sanctuary have glory, beauty (and color). Also, there are so many scriptures related to color in the Word. Since God has color, and it is in His sanctuary and His Word, then it seems appropriate to decorate our churches with pageantry that would be full of brilliance. The following is a list of colors, along with their significance and some corresponding scriptures. At the end, there is a simple-to-see chart for reiteration.

RAINBOW

Color spectrum (*Rainbow*) – contains all colors (Red, Orange, Yellow, Green, Blue, and Purple) and everything in between.

Genesis 9:16 – The rainbow shall be in the cloud, and I will look on it to remember the everlasting covenant between God and every living creature of all flesh that is on the earth.

Genesis 9:13 – I set My rainbow in the cloud, and it shall be for the sign of the covenant between Me and the earth.

Genesis 9:16

Revelation 4:3

RED

Offering, sacrifice, expiation (making amends), redemption, love, earth, life, devotion, war, atoning blood of Jesus, cleansing justification, flame, fire, blood, propitiation, scarlet, sin, consuming fire.

Is. 1:18 – Come now, and let us reason together, says the Lord, though your sins are like scarlet, they shall be as white as snow; though they are red like crimson, they shall be as wool.

Joshua 2:18, 21
Leviticus 14:52
Exodus 26:1
Acts 2:3

SARDIUS

(Carnelian, deep red) - Passion, righteous indignation, wrath, avenging fury, anger

Revelation 4:3 – And He who sat there was like a jasper and a sardius stone in appearance; and there was a rainbow around the throne, in appearance like an emerald.

Exodus 28:17

I Chronicles 13:10

ROSE/PINK/RASPBERRY

Rose of Sharon, innocence, glory, Messiah, heart, heart of flesh, purity of heart, blessings.

Ezekiel 11:19 – Then I will give them one heart, and I will put a new spirit within them, and take the stony heart out of their flesh, and give them a heart of flesh.

WINE

New wine

Ephesians 5:18 – And do not be drunk with wine, in which is dissipation; but be filled with the Spirit.

FUCHSIA

Gladness, delight, exultation, compassion, joy, right relationships

Ezra 6:16 – Then the children of Israel, the priests and the Levites and the rest of the descendants of the captivity, celebrated the dedication of this house of God with joy.

ORANGE

(Part of rainbow) - Covenant, agreement, promise, bond, fire, rising sun, setting sun

Acts 2:3 – Then there appeared to them divided tongues, as of fire, and one sat upon each of them.

Genesis 9:13

Genesis 9:16

AMBER

Glory of God, passion, Heavenly Father's loving care, wisdom, temple of God, God's fiery throne, fire, emotion, judgement

Ezekiel 1:4 – Then I looked, and behold, a whirlwind was coming out of the north, a great cloud with raging fire engulfing itself; and brightness was all around it and radiating out of its midst like the color of amber, out of the midst of the fire.

Ezekiel 8:2
Daniel 7:9

YELLOW

(Part of rainbow) – Covenant, promise, bond, agreement, fire, rising sun, setting sun

Exodus 19:18 – Now Mount Sinai was completely in smoke, because the Lord descended upon it in fire. Its smoke ascended like the smoke of a furnace, and the whole mountain quaked greatly.

Genesis 9:13, 16
Acts 2:3

GOLD

Resplendence, honor, eminence, glory of God, sovereignty, majesty, righteousness, divine light, kingliness, trial by fire, testing, the Godhead, purification, refinement, eternal deity, mercy, righteousness

Exodus 37:2,6 – He overlaid it with pure gold inside and outside, and made a molding of gold all around it. Vs.6 - He also made the mercy seat of pure gold; two and a half cubits was its length and a cubit and a half its width.

Malachi 3:2

BRONZE

Fires of testing, tribulation, discernment, judgement upon sin, wisdom

Deuteronomy 32:22 – For a fire is kindled in My anger, and shall

burn to the lowest hell; It shall consume the earth with her increase, and set on fire the foundations of the mountains.

Isaiah 33:14

GREEN

Mercy, benevolence, forgiveness, prosperity, new beginning, eternal life, spiritual growth, life, restoration, healing, vigor, strength, freshness, alive, abundance, thriving

Psalm 92:14 – They shall still bear fruit in old age; They shall be fresh and flourishing

Psalm 52:8
Psalm 37:35
Genesis 9:13,16

EMERALD

(Green, the dominant color in a rainbow) – Compassion, mercy, forgiveness.

Revelation 4:3 – And He who sat there was like a jasper and a sardius stone in appearance; and there was a rainbow around the throne, in appearance like an emerald.
Genesis 9:13,16

TURQUOISE

New Jerusalem, blessing, river of God, sanctification, healing, Holy Spirit's life-giving flow, stream, outpouring

Psalm 36:8,9 – They are abundantly satisfied with the fullness of Your house, and You give them drink from the river of Your pleasures. Vs. 9 – For with You is the fountain of life; In Your light we see light.

Exodus 28:18
Revelation 21:2
Psalm46:4
Ezekiel 47:1-12

BLUE

Heaven, heavenly, Holy Spirit, reward, angelic, divine, divinity, divine inspiration, revealed God, sanctity, grace, love, the priesthood, authority, bravery, over comer, royalty, courage

Exodus 26:1 – Moreover you shall make the tabernacle with ten curtains woven of fine linen thread, and blue and purple and scarlet yarn; with artistic designs of cherubim you shall weave them.

Exodus 24:10
Numbers 15:38
Ezekiel 1:26
Genesis 9:13,16

PURPLE/ORCHID/LILAC

Royalty, kingliness, power, dominion, sovereignty, reign, kingship, majesty

Revelation 1:6 – And has made us kings and priests to His God and father, to Him be glory and dominion forever and ever.

John 19:2
Judges 8:26
Ex. 28:8

BLACK

Sin, power, affliction, calamity, destruction, famine, mourning, evil, humiliation, darkness, death

Lamentations 4:6 –The punishment of the iniqu-
ity of the daughter of my people is greater than the punishment of the sin of Sodom, which was overthrown in a moment, with no hand to help her!

Jeremiah 8:21
Zechariah 6:2
Malachi 3:14
Revelation 6:5
Isaiah 1:18
Genesis 1
Isaiah 45:8
Psalm 97:2
Psalm 18:9,11

SILVER

Redemption, divinity, righteousness, atonement, the Word of God, strengthened faith, trust, integrity, refinement, wisdom

Cronicles 28:14 – He gave gold by weight for things of gold, for all articles used in every kind of service; also silver for all articles of silver by weight, for all articles used in every kind of service.

Exodus 27:17
Isaiah 1:18

JASPER

(Diamond-like, crystalline) - Purity, holiness, the glory of God, purification, sanctification, blessings of God, truth, bride of Christ, innocence, goodness, justice

Revelation 21:10,11 – And he carried me away in the spirit to a great and high mountain, and showed me the great city, the holy Jerusalem, descending out of heaven from God, Vs. 11 – having the glory of God. Her light was like a most precious stone, like a jasper stone, clear as crystal.

Revelation 4:3

WHITE

Holiness, purity, glory, Holy Spirit, blessedness, faith, righteousness, triumph, festivity, salvation, light, the bride, joy, surrender, rapture, angels, saints, victory, peace

Daniel 7:9 – I watched till thrones were put in place, and the Ancient of Days was seated; His garment was white as snow, and the hair of His head was like pure wool. His throne was a fiery flame, its wheels a burning fire.

Ecclesiastes 9:8
Isaiah 1:18
Zechariah 6:3
Matthew 17:2
John 20:12
Acts 2:3
Ephesians 5:18
Revelation 1:6
Revelation 6:2
Revelation 19:8

You can now create processionals, props, and pageantry with many colors and meanings. These can now have revelatory definition as well as artistic design. They can be full of brilliance and the grandeur of His *beauty.*

red	sardius	pink	wine	fucia
Offering	passion	rose of sharon	New wine	gladness
sacrifice	righteous indignation	innocence		delight
expiation	wrath	glory		exultation
redemption	avenging fury	messiah		compassion
love	anger	heart of flesh		joy
earth		purity of heart		right relationships
life		blessings		
devotion				
war				
atoning blood of Jesus				
cleansing justification				
flame				
fire				
blood				
propitiation				
scarlet				
sin				
consuming fire				

orange	amber	yellow	gold	bronze
covenant	glory of God	covenant	resplendence	Fires of testing
agreement	passion	promise	honor	tribulation
promise	loving care	bond	eminence	discernment
bond	wisdom	agreement	glory of god	judgement of sin
fire	temple of God	fire	sovereignty	wisdom
rising sun	God's fiery throne	rising sun	majesty	
setting sun	fire	setting sun	righteousness	
	emotion		divine light	
	judgement		kingliness	
			trial by fire	
			godhead	
			purification	
			eternal deity	
			mercy	
			testing	
			refinement	

green	emerald	turquoise	blue
mercy	compassion	new jerusalem	heaven
benebolence	mercy	blessing	heavenly
forgiveness	forgiveness	river of god	holy spirit
prosperity		sanctification	reward
new beginning		healing	angelic
eternal life		life giving flow	divine
life		stream	divinity
restoration		outpouring	divine inspiration
healing			revealed god
vigor			sanctity
strength			grace
freshness			love
alive			Priesthood
abundance			Authority
thriving			Overcomer
spiritual growth			Royalty
			Courage
			Bravery

purple/ orchid	black	silver	Jasper	white
royalty	sin	redemption	purity	holiness
kingliness	affliction	divinity	holiness	purity
power	calamity	righteousness	glory of God	glory
dominion	destruction	atonement	blessings of God	holy spirit
sovereignty	famine	word of God	purification	blessedness
reign	mourning	strengthened faith	sanctification	faith
kingship	evil	trust	truth	righteousness
majesty	humiliation	integrity	bride of christ	triumph
	darkness	wisdom	innocence	festivity
	death	refinement	goodness	salvation
	power		justice	light
				the bride
				joy
				surrender
				rapture
				angels
				saints
				victory
				peace

Scriptural Significance

Chapter 10: faith in a "material" world

Hebrews 11:1 – Now faith is the substance of things hoped for and the evidence of things not seen.

Faith is a funny thing. It has substance and evidence, neither of which are tangible until it happens. Something you have always wanted or hoped for (within God's will) and things that you have never seen will happen through activation of something you can not touch.
We live in a very tangible and *materialistic* world (of which we need not be a part) that tells us '*seeing* is believing'; '*feel* the difference quality makes'; 'it is a *taste* sensation'; '*smell* the freshness'; 'experience *sound* distinction'. All these sensorial messages try to steer us away from faith.
Can a piece of *material* heal the sick? Can someone *passing by* cause deliverance? Is it something tangible or intangible that causes a miracle to happen? These next few scriptures should help answer some of these questions.

Luke 8:44,48 – came from behind and touched the border (hem) of His garment. And immediately her flow of blood stopped. Vs. 48 And He said to her, "Daughter, be of good cheer; your ***faith*** *has made you well. Go in peace."*

Matthew 14:35-36 – And when the men of that place recognized Him, they sent out into all that surrounding region, brought to Him all who were sick, Vs. 36 and begged Him that they might only touch the hem of His garment. And as many as touched it were made perfectly well.

In both of these instances, these people had enough faith to believe that if they could just touch the hem of his garment they could be healed. Does this mean that there is power in a cotton robe? Should we all run out and make garments like those that Jesus wore? That is absurd! Jesus points out to the woman with the issue of blood that it was not the hem of the garment that made her well, but her *faith.* What significance, then does the robe have? If all she needed to do was believe, then why did she have to touch a tangible object? The tassels on the edge of the robe could have reminded her (a Jewish woman) of the Torah. It also could have been a visible point of contact for faith activation.

Matthew 20:30 – And behold, two blind men sitting by the road, when they heard that Jesus was ***passing by,*** *cried out, saying, "Have mercy on us, O Lord, Son of David!"*

John 9:1&7 – Now as Jesus ***passed by,*** *He saw a man who was blind from birth. Vs. 7 And He said to him, "Go, wash in the pool of Siloam." So he went and washed, and came back seeing.*

Acts 5:15-16 – So that they brought the sick out into the streets and laid them on beds and couches, that at least the ***shadow***

***of Peter passing by** might fall on some of them. Vs. 16 Also a multitude gathered from the surrounding cities to Jerusalem, bringing sick people and those who were tormented by unclean spirits, and they were all healed.*

Both Jesus and Peter (meaningful and tangible points of contact between the natural and the supernatural) ***passed by*** the needy, stirring them to action. In each instance, the people took some kind of action toward their healing or deliverance. There was a glimmer of hope that their unseen healing would soon be evident.

One time we had a long row of people at the front of the sanctuary. Behind them was a long row of people waving large (3'X 3') flags (over their heads). Three dancers moved (*passed by*) back and forth in front of them, and a song about deliverance was playing in the background. We experienced a sovereign move of God that was unparalleled. Many people cried out, some fell to their knees weeping, and others went through deliverance. We did not lay hands on anyone.

The dancers moving back and forth in front of the line of people may have caused faith activation like Jesus did when He passed by those in need. The flags over head could have been the visible, tangible points of contact necessary to release enough faith for healing and deliverance. Who knows, maybe if the light was just right, the flags might have cast a shadow like Peter's. In either case, dancers, flags and shadows do not actually perform miracles. It is *faith* in God through the power of the Holy Spirit. Please keep this in mind as you hear more testimonies (in chapter 12) about how God miraculously moved during our use of cloths and props.

Practical Guide

Chapter 11: Creative costuming

Exodus 28:2-3 – "And you shall make holy (sacred) garments for Aaron your brother, for glory and for beauty. Vs. 3 So you shall speak to all who are gifted artisans, whom I have filled with the spirit of wisdom, that they may make Aaron's garments, to consecrate him, that he may minister to Me as priest."

"Aaron's garments were different from those of the others because he was the highest representative. All others were subordinate to him. As high priest, Aaron was Israel's chief representative before God; conversely, he was God's representative before the people. Aaron was a type of Christ, who is our High Priest." [2]

The rest of chapter 28 goes on to describe in accurate detail, the marvelous splendor, colorful array and wondrous beauty of his garments. These were to be hand crafted, with utmost care, so it would be "presentation ready" for the King of Kings!

Appropriate costume selection is almost as important to the dance as the choreography itself! We as priests, have many things to consider while preparing a costume to be presentation ready. We have an awesome calling and responsibility to minister to the King of Kings. Let us look at some topics with respect to **creative costuming**.

HOW TO BUILD A FUNCTIONAL, INTERCHANGEABLE WARDROBE FROM SCRATCH

Practically speaking, a lot of costuming depends on your budget. It can be done quite inexpensively, if necessary. When I first started dancing with a team back in the mid 80's, we each paid for our own costumes that the team seamstress made. Sometimes, when a new person would join the team, she would borrow a costume from someone who was no longer on the team (until she could build her own wardrobe).

In the 90's when I was the assistant dance leader at another church, we started with nothing but white skirts that we had borrowed from other church members and just about everyone had some kind of black pants. Afterwards, the church mercifully gave us $100.00 to go out and buy some material. We bought enough yardage of white lining material to make eight white worship dresses. A few of us spent several days in the Sunday school room, with portable sewing machines and commenced stitching. We were so proud of our accomplishments that were definitely a step up from borrowed skirts. These belonged to the church dance/ drama department and after laundering (which I usually did), stayed in the appropriate closet. We then began adding accessories to change the look for a particular dance such as: Red satin vests for songs related to the blood; reversible gold/purple vests representing glory/ royalty; gold belts, headbands, wristbands for glory or warfare; etc. We wore them for every presentation for a few years. We then ventured out and made white satin pants and shirts, to which we added the same accessories. As time wore on, we got tired of white. People of all shapes and sizes began to join the team (so the selection of dresses or pants did not always fit everyone) and people, in general, were not taking care of their borrowed church garments.

Finally, we decided that it was time to branch out and try incorporating some color. Meanwhile, we prayed for a seamstress who had a heart and call to out-fit the dance team. We did and she came! From then on, we had a variety explosion. We transitioned from the white worship dresses to white silk essence circle skirts (as a base) with white over lays (a simple front and back panel-type top that wraps and ties). Skirts a little shorter then ankle length work best for mobility and agility especially when having to get up from a kneeling position. We then progressed to various colored skirts and overlays. As people would join the team, we would ask them to purchase their own costumes (or at least pay the seamstress to make it for them) and be responsible for their care. This proved to be very successful. After a while, the seamstress would announce that silk essence was on sale. If any one wanted to put in an order for a circle skirt, she would purchase the material in bulk.

Over the years, the team had so many interchangeable skirt and over lay combinations that we had to have a costume schedule for praise and worship. Since not everybody had every color, it took quite a bit of planning to coordinate who was dancing on what day and who had what colors. We set up a schedule that looked something like:

Week 1 - Blue and white
Week 2 – Purple, gold and white
Week 3 - Any color bottom, white top
Week 4 – All white any color belt

The men that eventually joined the team simply wore white pants, shirts, shoes and socks and accessories (sash, vest, etc.) to match everyone else. Almost everyone had white by this time so, even if they were new to the team and had not built up their personal wardrobe yet, we could always find the appropriate color belt or overlay for them to blend. When you make your belts, sashes, vests, overlays, and tunics, it is a good idea to make them reversible. This at least doubles your choice variety! More recently, we discovered that tunics (thigh-length, vest-type over shirts that are usually made of silk essence or any “flowy” material) are wonderful. They cover all the places we want covered, can be easily worn over skirts, dresses, or pants, and we do not have concern ourselves with whether or not it is coming “un-tucked.” We did require that the ladies eventually purchase a white, long sleeved leotard, white culottes, pink tights and pink ballet shoes (especially if they felt called to the dance ministry). There was always a sufficient grace period where they could wear a white turtle neck or cotton top with white stockings from the local grocery store, and white bedroom slippers. However, if it looked like they were ready to make a serious commitment, we strongly recommended the purchase of the appropriate attire. This always worked very well for us. When it came time to do a special presentation piece, there was more then enough selection from which to choose.

Other churches have their own method or format. One very successful costume plan is that if you join the team, you must have a white base for Sunday worship and a black base for the mid-week service.

White base

White long-sleeve leotard
White sports bra
Pink ballet tights
Pink ballet slippers
White stretch pants *(under a skirt)*
White pants *(optional)*

Black base

Black long-sleeve leotard
Black sports bra
Black tights
Black jazz shoes
Black stretch pants *(under a skirt)*
Black pants *(loose fitting pants no matter what color are wonderful for ease of movement, getting up and down from the floor, and you do not need to wear as many layers)*

The church then provides the matching shirts and belts. They look for a group of shirts on sale at a discount department store and buy six to eight of them

in varying sizes. The idea of the two types of bases is outstanding and simple.
I hope that this will have given you some ideas from which you may get started and build your dance team wardrobe.

TAKING PRECAUTION

I would like to mention a few things that we should watch (some "DON'TS" if you will). Since we house the Holy Ghost, we want to draw attention to the Spirit resident within and not its temple. Therefore, taking these precautionary measures will assist us in achieving that goal.

Modesty

A good sports bra is especially important. Check yourself at home to be sure that nothing moves and you can not see anything through your costume. This includes bra straps (if you do not have a sports bra yet), panty lines (if you do not have a leotard yet), and leotard lines. Watch that the costume is not too tight especially if it is cotton knit type material. Be sure that the shirt or blouse is not too low cut. We want the congregation to look at the Creator not on His creation. It is also much easier to dance if you do not have to be concerned about this. A good jewel neck leotard should take care of that problem.

Wrong Size

It is just as important that you have the right size costume. If it is too tight, it could be uncomfortable and prohibit movement. On the other hand, if it is too large, it could feel awkward, look sloppy, and be distracting. Try to have costumes made that fit well enough to have unrestricted freedom of movement and you will be well pleased.

Culottes vs. Stretch Pants

There is no rule written in stone, but I highly recommend wearing culottes under a circle skirt or dress. Any fabric store carries this common pattern. Culottes the same color as your dress or skirt work best, but sometimes gold lame' or pearl essence is good for effect. Dark colors under light skirts are usually ineffectual. Culottes work well because they: flow with your skirt, keep your legs covered, do not cling to your leg, and do not ride up when your skirt flares during a spin. Stretchy pants will suffice, but they are somewhat like thick tights. If your skirt flares, the audience sees the shape of your legs and such. Yes, the skin may be covered, but the outline is obvious. Some may feel that choosing culottes over stretch pants is taking a prudish stance. However, when we are dancing in front of people for the Lord, we want the focus to be on His glory radiating from our faces, not our leg shape flashing from our skirts.

Disrepair

Watch for hanging strings, rips or holes (in your costume, tights or shoes), and excessive wrinkles.

Jewelry

The many years of ballet training indelibly taught me not to wear any jewelry at all. With the exception of a wedding ring and maybe very tiny stud earrings, we were restricted from wearing any kind of adornments. The reasoning of the professional dance schools was so the audience would be able to focus on the fluidity of the movement and smooth body lines. Necklaces, watches, bracelets, etc. could distract from movement and break those lines. Though worship dancers are not as overly concerned about body lines (since we are relatively covered up), we *are* concerned about the audience's focus. Like the professional dancer, we do not want anything to distract. Therefore, though we may not need to be as strict as the professionals (use good judgement and taste), we want to keep in mind that our audience is viewing and experiencing the anointing and Glory of God.

Nails and Hair

The same philosophy holds true for fingernails, toenails, and hair. If there is a group of dancers on the stage all doing a very simple hand movement up and down, but one woman has on bright red nail polish, guess on what the audience's eye will rivet. Likewise, long hair, if it is not secured, (most of the time) will draw attention to itself.

Chewing Gum

Although gum is not a part of a costume or wardrobe, I thought it fitting to insert this tip: ***do not chew gum*** during praise and worship, presentations, or in dance class. Not only is it hazardous to your health, but it is very distracting to anyone watching you.

White Tights vs. Pink

I discovered quite some time ago that though the difference may be slight, white legs against a dark back drop look stockier. Pink tights seem to create softer, less noticeable lines. I should mention here, that your shoes should match your tights. Enough said.

Labels and Facing

If you do happen to purchase your shirts from a store, be sure to either take out the label or stitch it down. Sometimes a label can be seen through the material or stick out somewhere. In either case, it could be a minor distraction that should be fixed. Likewise, if your costume is hand made and has facing or interfacing, be sure it is tacked down.

At any rate, whatever the cause, we should minimize distractions. Let the focus be on the giver of life, and the life-giving message, not on the message's messenger!

PURPOSEFUL COSTUMING FOR DANCES AND PROCESSIONALS

It is possible for the costumes in a particular presentation, to be as meaningful as the interpretive choreography. In some cases, the costuming adds meaningful purpose to the dances and processionals. We will look at examples from the obvious to the marvelous.

As you learned in chapter 9, there are many symbolic meanings for a variety of colors. Many of these are easy for the audience to interpret. For instance, if one half of the team were dressed in black and the other half in white, you could pretty well deduce what they represent.

The black half could represent evil, demons or sin, and the white half could represent angels, righteousness, or goodness. If there were some kind of conflict between them, it would be safe to assume that represents spiritual warfare. These would be appropriate garment and colors for such an occasion. Pants are particularly good for this type of dance interpretation because there is usually some kind of representative combat for which you would need mobility and sprightliness. Obviously, if the 'bad guys' came out in pastel pink or lavender dresses, the audience would be scratching their heads (wondering what the dance is trying to say). Alternatively, if the 'good guys' came out in shiny black vinyl or brown velvet pants, it would probably evoke the same type of response.

We did a dance about the refiner's fire, once. At the time, we still had our "basic whites," so the flag ministry leader suggested that we very simply add fire-colored ribbons. We tied one long red ribbon around our waist onto which we slip-knotted several 18" or so red, yellow, orange and gold ribbons. They were evenly distributed around the waist, so when we twirled, they flared out somewhat, creating a 'fiery' effect. She also made headbands with interwoven twists of red and yellow material and gold trim. We used those costumes over again in another dance to which we added red and yellow overlays and flags (with the same colors on them).

When we did the dance "What Sin," the ones who played the part of sin and torment, eventually ended up in the sea of forgetfulness (which as I mentioned earlier, was a blue five-yard silk essence cloth). They wore blue overlays, white pants, white leotards, and were barefoot. I, the one tormented, wore all white with a gold sash, and the woman who played God wore a white dress with a gold vest. Looking back, we were probably more concerned with matching each other and the sea then what a more appropriate color choice might have been. At that time, we were limited by what we had on hand.

If I were to do it all over again, I probably would have put the tormenters in a black base with a blue overlay. I probably would have put myself in blue pants with a white overlay or tunic, and put God in white pants and a white tunic with gold trim (to be in keeping with the rest of us in pants). Most of the time, we worked with what we all had and not necessarily what worked best for interpretation.

I did see however, an excellent example of purposeful, interpretive costuming at one of our conferences. The song was "My Deliverer" to which several dancers wore solid colored tops and matching bottoms, although different from one another. They were purposely different, however. Part way through the dance, each one of them took turns going to another person who was covered under some type of large, dark cloth. They individually proceeded to unveil, unwrap, or uncover the ones who were symbolically oppressed which revealed that they were dressed identically. Each one was introduced to their deliverer and set free! It was captivating and surprising. A lady, who had been waiting on the stage (observing all the dramatic salvations), was dressed just like a Jewish man. At the end of the song, she walked slowly across the stage toward the cross, picked up the 'sackcloth' type cloths that had been removed from the oppressed, looked at them and dropped them in disgust. She then reached for the long red cloth that was loosely draped on the cross. While realizing that Jesus was her Messiah, she held the cloth close, fell to her knees, and wept. The whole dance ministered and was a powerful multi-level portrayal with excellent use of interpretive costuming.

Another dance done at the same conference was "New Jerusalem." Without going into detail about the ongoing resurgence of anointing and eye catching splendor, there were also purposeful costumes throughout. The ones that stand out were the dancers in white skirts and tunics, which were adorned with turquoise neck pieces. These were circular type collars that (I assume) snapped or Velcro in the back, which covered their shoulders and chest. They also carried turquoise props that were rather unusual. Of course, you know that after reading the color chapter, turquoise represents the New Jerusalem. The audience might have just observed it as a lovely color if they did not have the deeper revelation or knowledge that turquoise had that particular interpretation. However, in this case, it was not hard to figure out because both the music and the movements so well explained the song. The whole dance was wonderful.

Processionals, on the other hand, at least in my opinion, look good and minister well, when the main corps of dancers looks identical. One thing that makes processionals unique and different from a dramatic dance is the uniform simplicity. Another thing that stands out about processionals is the inclusion of a large number of people worshipping in unity. When the priests of old brought up the ark, gave thanks and worshipped in one accord, the glory of the Lord was so evident, the priests could not stand. Likewise, when there is unity in movement and dress, it has an awesome effect. That does not discount the times where extravagant royal pageantry is in perfect order with a multitudinous blend of purple, blue, and gold. Let us not overlook the times of joyous celebration when the occasion calls for glorious brilliant colors. Dare I not mention the seasonal celebrations where rich, red Christmas velvet would be warming to the heart? We should never get stuck in a mold that could get ever so stifling.

With scriptural knowledge of significant color symbolism, combined with creative choreography, the possibilities for costuming with meaningful purpose are vast. This can beautifully aid in ministering to the hearts of people and gloriously aid in ministering (as Aaron did) to the Lord.

Practical Guide

Chapter 12: Ministry Palette

Song Of Solomon 6:4 – Oh, my love, you are as beautiful as Tizah, lovely as Jerusalem, awesome as an army with banners!

While exalting her beauty, power, and majesty as Queen, she is compared to some of the best and most precious things conceivable. To be awesome as an army with banners is quite a compliment. We can only imagine the overwhelming sense of awe that comes from the sight of hundreds of representative flags blowing in the wind. With the knowledge that the army that bears them is marching in one accord to battle for the country which it represents. To both the viewer of the army and the viewer of the Queen, the overall beauty of the beheld touches them deeply.

We too, as both creators of design and observers of beauty can allow God to use us as artists. He can give us a stage for an easel, movement for a canvas, and an unlimited palette of dancing color and design. His masterpiece when presented to the masses may minister profoundly and change their lives.

CREATING PROP DESIGNS

I did a workshop, one time where we created a huge processional spontaneously. The purpose was to not only teach about impromptu creativity, but also how to put together a processional using props. Unfortunately, so I thought, we did not have any props. A little on-the-spot ingenuity suggested that we just pretend. So I assigned *imaginary* banners, flags, streamers, scarves and hoops to various people. I quickly placed them in the appropriate places and we then practiced timing and execution. It went extremely well and there was a powerful anointing. We were all very excited about our one-hour accomplishment and opted to repeat it several times.

The next workshop, I repeated the same exercise, only this time there were twice as many people, and at least that many props. The basic impromptu construction went fairly well, however, there were just too many props! Fortunately, these were just exercises for learning and not stage-ready presentations. We had just about every kind of prop you could imagine (including flowered arches, which work beautifully in a procession). We had fun putting it all together, but I taught them that as extravagant as this may appear, even the most splendid pageants need to be done in good taste with appropriate design. I told them that although we were able to think inventively and spontaneously, I would recommend many more rehearsals to adjust and readjust spacing, timing and placement.

When preparing processionals (or any type dance for that matter), keep in mind these few fundamentals:

Projected Picture

Think like an artist painting a scene. There should be good design with varying levels, shapes, dynamics and colors.

Visual Coordination

If you are using a variety of props to interpret the song, try not to haphazardly scatter them around only to 'pop up' or be used when their part comes up in the song. This is a type of 'Micky-Mousing' the music. 'Micky-Mousing' the music is when you literally interpret every single word to a song (almost like literal sign language). This gets too overrun and it is hard for the audience to keep up.

Prop Number

Too many may look busy or confusing. The introduction of too many types of props may lend itself to being gaudy and distracting. If you have a row of hoops, a row of flags, a row of laurels, a row of hand banners, and a row of finger streamers, it may just be too much for the audience to look at. I would either narrow down the selection altogether, or have them enter and exit at different times during the song.

Prop Relativity

How props relate to one another is important. If you have two rows, let us say of different kinds of props, have their movements be somewhat coordinated (not necessarily identical). For instance, in the example I used earlier in "Ancient of Days," the choreographer had the back row interpreting the base guitar music with a very simple movement using laurels while the other instrument interpretations moved across in front of them. It was very appealing and interesting to watch.

Color Scheme

Scriptural significance would be good, but if you are just going for color, it is good to have some kind of palette uniformity. In other words, do not have 5 purple flags, 5 blue flags, 5 red flags and *one orange one.*

Song Theme

If the song is about the Blood of Jesus, go ahead and use red props – pink or yellow just will not do!

Message

Think about how the message illustration will relate to the audience. Make sure they can read and understand your visual concepts. Do not make the interpretative movement or props so deep that it would take a submarine crew of theologians to figure it out. Incorporating a small portion of drama as an introduction (before the music begins) is a nice enhancement.

Number of People

Space them out well. Work on entrance and exit timing. Design their placement with variety in mind. Do not over crowd a small area with too many people. Spread them out, put them on different levels, fill the sanctuary, and use the aisles (as well as the front and steps). Do not be afraid to create "Surround Sound" with "Anointing Around!"

Symmetry/Asymmetry

When using large props, especially, it is nice to have symmetry. If you have huge banners or flags, put one on each side of the front. If you have an even number of flags, put half on one side, half on the other side. If you have an odd number, do the same, only have the remaining odd number one(s) in the middle (perhaps doing a different movement). Symmetrical design is also nice to use when you have a large number of props.

Allow God to use you as an artist to create splendor and beauty fit for a King and pleasant to the eye of the beholder. Let your spirit-inspired creations minister to the hearts of men and touch the heart of God. Then watch God move through your pageantry!

WATCHING GOD MINISTER THROUGH PAGEANTRY

Several times, we have experienced a mighty move of God, using props during pageantry filled dances. We can literally sense His presence and experience healing during their use. There is no magic in silk essence or wizardry in worship cloths. The anointing of the Holy Spirit flowing through a faith-filled (sometimes banner bearing) believer is where God does the work and gets all the glory!

At Christian Retreat, in Bradenton, Florida, the Feast of Tabernacles is held annually. There is a woman there who creates the most spectacular, awe-inspiring banners and she usually gives banner making classes during the Feast. One year, I remember watching one of the banners that was among the many spread across the front of the sanctuary. As it was gently waving forward and back, I could tangibly feel waves of anointing pouring forth. It really ministered. It is so awesome when the right truth-bearing banner comes forth by the unction of the Holy Spirit. This can even change the whole flow of a service where ministry can take place.

Countless testimonies have been given about how the use of flags has ministered healing, deliverance, and peace. When we presented "Spirit of the Sovereign Lord," two men carried very large flags throughout the dance. This one part, where the music increased in intensity, they went from the front of the sanctuary to the back, boldly waving their flags over the congregation. Everyone sensed God's presence as the flags bejeweled anointing over his or her head.

During another segment of the same dance, we carried gold lame' cloths *over* the congregation. They represented the Spirit of the sovereign Lord being upon them, His glory and presence, as well as all the favor He bestowed in Isaiah 61:1. As they went over, sounds of weeping were heard throughout the sanctuary, and people fell out under the power of the Holy Spirit. Upon completion of the dance, there was an unsolicited altar call where people voluntarily labored through the density of God's presence to arrive at the front for ministry. It was powerful.

There have been several occasions where we have literally used props during ministry. One time, we wrapped a woman up in a gold cloth. We then had her unravel herself while I held the loose end of the cloth. The cloth not only represented God's glory, presence, covering and protection, but also an unraveling and stripping away of the old tangling torment. She was set free through faith.

One gentleman came to our meeting who was obviously oppressed. He wanted to be set free and had faith to believe. We wrapped him up in a red lame' cloth (symbolizing the blood of Jesus). The demons could not stand that so they fled. There was a dramatic deliverance and he is a different person today!

One of the most awesome testimonies is about healing. During one of our "normal" dance practice times, we had a little message and ministry before the meeting. To make a long story short, there was a long red cloth spread out on the floor and a gold cloth folded up in a two foot by two foot square. Without repeating the entire corresponding message, the people knelt down and prayed at the red cloth (the cleansing blood of Jesus), then stood on the square (God's glory). Once they experienced a touch from God, they were encouraged to cross over into His rest. Everyone experienced something tangibly, but one person was touched miraculously. While she was standing on the gold cloth, I could see a manifestation of the Holy Spirit as she bent over not withstanding His presence. She went to the other side and fell out under the power. She lay there for quite some time.

We knew that she had a powerful encounter with the Almighty. It was not until the next evening at service that we heard her testimony. Only one week before, she had been diagnosed with a breast tumor. The morning after our "normal" dance practice and her experience on the gold cloth, she went to the doctor who reported that there was not one trace of the tumor anywhere! A thunderous praise to God commenced, and He got all the glory!

The testimonies could go on for pages and days, but suffice it to say that God moves through art (no matter what the Spirit-filled medium). We can *build* a splendor rich pageant, filled with awe and wonderment. We can *create* a processional with resplendent glory and majesty. We can *choreograph* a dance that touches the soul of man. However, it is the Lord who gives us the tools with which to *build*, the ingenuity with which to *create*, and the methods by which to *choreograph*. Therefore, ministering to Him makes the presentation as beautiful as Tizah, lovely as Jerusalem, and awesome as an army with banners!

Conclusion

Reading and learning about the scriptural significance and practical aspects of processionals, props and pageantry, is only the beginning. Endless forms of aesthetic and artistic expression are available. With prayer, planning, practice and props, you can create a masterpiece for the Master that is worth all the time and effort. With creative costuming and a colorfully arrayed ministry palette, you can design a glorious processional, for the King, presented with an entirety of majestic brilliance. Not only is it a sweet smelling fragrance to Him, but also can be dramatic, life-changing ministry to its recipients! May your creativity be stirred, and your pageantry shine!

Bibliography

[1] *The Exhaustive Concordance of the Bible*
Abingdon Press, Nashville Forty-second Printing 1983
James Strong Madison, N.J.
Key Word Comparison © 1980 by Abingdon

[2] *Spirit Filled Life Bible – New King James Version Scripture quotations and some comments*
Thomas Nelson Publishers – Nashville – Atlanta – London – Vancouver
Thomas Nelson, Inc. ©1991
General Editor – Jack W. Hayford, Litt. D.
Old Testament Editor – Sam Middlebrook, D. Min.
New Testament Editor – Jerry Horner, Th.D.
Assistant Editor – Gary Mastdorf, M.S.

[3] *Webster's New World Dictionary of the American Language*
Simon and Schuster, a division of Gulf and Western Corp. ©1982
1230 Avenue of the Americas New York, New York 10020

[4] *The American Heritage Dictionary of the English Language*
© 1969,1970 American Heritage Publishing Co., Inc.
551 Fifth Avenue, New York, New York 10017
William Morris, Editor

dancing For Him

MISSION STATEMENT

Dancing For Him is a biblically based, spirit filled organization whose purpose is to minister healing and deliverance to people's hearts through creative expressions of worship, prophesy, and dance. As artistic ministers who transcribe the heart of God into an acceptable life changing form, we exist to teach others about this unique art form through which to spread the gospel of Jesus Christ and set captives free!

Dancing For Him Worship Dance conferences are only phase I of a Five-Phase plan. This is to: minister, train, and activate others to effectively reach the lost; heal the sick, wounded and broken hearted; and open prison doors to those who are bound. During these awe-inspiring conferences, technical dance training is obtained; but more important, an impartation of anointing to minister through music and dance is transmitted. Please visit our Web site to see the other phases

FOR FURTHER INFORMATION ABOUT:

- Attending one of our conferences
- Having us minister at your church
- Hosting a workshop in your area
- Ordering books, DVDs & videos
- Getting on our mailing list

Please feel free to contact us at:
www.dancingforhim.com